Intermediate Paper 8

Management Accou
– Performance Man

GW01099455

First edition 2002
Third edition January 2004

ISBN 0 7517 1489 5 (previous edition 0 7517 0266 8)

British Library Cataloguing-in-Publication Data

A catalogue record for this book is available from the British Library

Published by

BPP Professional Education, Aldine House, Aldine Place, London W12 8AW

www.bpp.com

Printed in Great Britain by Ashford Colour Press

Welcome to BPP's CIMA **Passcards** for Paper 8 *Management Accounting – Performance Management*.

- They **save you time**. Important topics are summarised for you.

- They incorporate **diagrams** to kick start your memory.

- They follow the overall **structure** of the BPP Study Texts, but BPP's CIMA **Passcards** are not just a condensed book. Each card has been separately designed for clear presentation. Topics are self contained and can be grasped visually.

- CIMA **Passcards** are still **just the right size** for pockets, briefcases and bags.

- CIMA **Passcards** **focus on the exam** you will be facing.

Run through the complete set of **Passcards** as often as you can during your final revision period. The day before the exam, try to go through the **Passcards** again! You will then be well on your way to passing your exams.

Good luck!

1: Standard costing

Topic List

As well as providing a brief reminder of the basics of the topic covered in your earlier studies, this chapter looks at the higher-level Paper 8 standard costing issues such as behavioural implications.

Refer to MCQ cards (with Ch 2):   1-27

Situations in which standard costing can be used

- Batch/mass production and process manufacture
- Jobbing manufacture (if there is standardisation of parts)
- Service industries (if there is a realistic cost unit)

> Although it can be used in a variety of costing situations, the greatest benefit from standard costing can be gained if there is a degree of repetition in the production process (mass production and repetitive assembly work).

Note that a standard cost per task can be calculated if there is a similarity of tasks. In this way standard costing can be used by some service organisations.

Uses of standard costing

- **To act as a control device (variance analysis)**
- **To value stocks and cost production**
- To assist in setting budgets and evaluating managerial performance
- To enable the principle of 'management by exception' to be practised
- To provide a prediction of future costs for use in decision-making situations
- To motivate staff and management by providing challenging targets
- To provide guidance on possible ways of improving efficiency

Allowing for inflation in material and labour cost standards

- Use of current price as standard produces constantly increasing adverse variances.
- Use of an estimated mid-year price produces favourable variances in the first half of the year, adverse variances in the second half.

Evolution and continuous improvement

- A standard needs to evolve over a few accounting periods before it can be used as a useful measure for control purposes.
- Standards can be continuously improved by refined/increased standard-setting procedures or revision of standards.

Types of performance standard

Ideal
- Perfect operating conditions
- Unfavourable motivational impact

Attainable
- Allowances made for inefficiencies and wastage
- Incentive to work harder (realistic but challenging)

Current
- Based on current working conditions
- No motivational impact

Basic
- Unaltered over a long period of time
- Unfavourable impact on performance

1: Standard costing

Setting standards for overheads

Standard absorption rate (predetermined OAR) depends on planned **production volume**, which depends on two factors:

production capacity (in standard hours of output) and **efficiency** of working.

Capacity can be **full**, **practical** or **budgeted**.

Example

A work force consists of 20 men, who each work a 35 hour week.

The standard time per unit = $2\frac{1}{2}$ hours and expected efficiency of the workforce = 125%.

Budgeted capacity = $20 \times 35 = 700$ production hrs/wk.

The work force should take 1 hour to produce 1.25 ($1 \times 125\%$) standard hours of output.

Budgeted output = $700 \times 125\% = 875$ standard hours of output per week.

Budgeted production volume = $875 \div 2\frac{1}{2} = 350$ units of output per week.

Capacity ratios

Production volume ratio = capacity ratio × efficiency ratio

$$\frac{\text{Actual output in std hrs}}{\text{Budged capacity}} = \frac{\text{Actual hrs worked}}{\text{Budgeted capacity}} \times \frac{\text{Actual output in std hrs}}{\text{Actual hrs worked}}$$

A standard costing system will only be effective if it is designed with full understanding of its potential behavioural effects.

Effect 1 Different types of performance standard have different effects (see earlier).

Effect 2 Communication is of the utmost importance (to win the support of production employees and their supervisors and to incorporate their practical knowledge).

Effect 3 The variance reporting system should not be used punitively. There must be no undue pressure or excessive blame attached to the non-achievement of standards, otherwise it will cause resentment and the standard costing system will be less effective.

Effect 4 There is a need to distinguish between controllable and uncontrollable costs to ensure managers are not demotivated by being held responsible for costs/variances they cannot control.

Effect 5 Variance control reports should be produced promptly and accurately: late information may cause frustration if managers feel that they could have acted earlier if they had known that problems existed; inaccuracy will lead to managers losing faith in the value of the information and they may not bother to act upon it.

Effect 6 Standards set should encourage goal congruence between individuals and the organisation as a whole.

1: Standard costing

Similarities

They both involve looking to the future and forecasting what is likely to happen given a certain set of circumstances.

They are both used for control purposes.

Interrelationships

A standard unit cost of production can act as the basis for a production cost budget: standard unit cost × budgeted activity level = budgeted expenditure.

Differences

A budget gives the planned total aggregate costs for a function or cost centre whereas a standard shows unit resource usage and cost.

Standards can only be used where actions are performed and output can be measured, whereas budgets can be prepared for all functions, even when output cannot be measured.

2: Variance analysis

Topic List

Variable cost variances

Fixed overhead variances (non-graphical)

Fixed overhead variances (graphical)

Sales variances

Variance analysis is one of the key techniques that you are required to master for this paper. Be aware of the similarities in the calculation and meaning of the variable cost variances (material, labour, variable overhead) and remember that the fixed overhead variances are attempting to explain the under/over absorption of fixed overheads.

Key question to try in the kit: 10
Refer to MCQ cards (with Ch 1):   1-27

Example to be used throughout this chapter

Standard cost of product A	£
Materials (5 kgs × £10 per kg)	50
Labour (4 hrs × £5 per hour)	20
Variable o/hds (4 hrs × £2 per hour)	8
Fixed o/hds (4 hrs × £6 per hour)	24
	102

Actual results	
Production	1,000 units
Sales	900 units
Materials	4,850 kgs, £46,075
Labour	4,200 hrs, £21,210
Variable o/hds	£9,450
Fixed o/hds	£25,000
Selling price	£140 per unit

Budgeted results	
Production	1,200 units
Sales	1,000 units
Selling price	£150 per unit

Direct material total variance

The difference between what the output actually cost, and what it should have cost, in terms of material

This can be divided into two sub-variances.

Direct material price variance

The difference between what the material used did cost and what it should have cost

Direct material usage variance

The difference between the standard cost of the material that should have been used and the standard cost of the material that was used

Example	
	£
1,000 units should have cost (× £50)	50,000
but did cost	46,075
Direct material total variance	3,925 (F)
	£
4,850 kgs should have cost (× £10)	48,500
but did cost	46,075
Direct material price variance	2,425 (F)
1,000 units should have used (× 5 kgs)	5,000 kgs
but did use	4,850 kgs
Variance in kgs	150 kgs (F)
× standard cost per kg	× £10
Direct material usage variance	£1,500 (F)

Direct labour total variance

The difference between what the output actually cost and what it should have cost, in terms of labour

Again this can be divided into two sub-variances.

Direct labour rate variance

The difference between what the labour used did cost and what it should have cost

Direct labour efficiency variance

The difference between the standard cost of the hours that should have been worked and that standard cost of the hours that were worked. When idle time occurs, the efficiency variance is based on hours actually worked (not hours paid for) and an **idle time variance** (hours of idle time × standard rate per hour) is calculated.

Example

	£
1,000 units should have cost (× £20)	20,000
but did cost	21,210
Direct labour total variance	1,210 (A)

	£
4,200 hrs should have cost (× £5)	21,000
but did cost	21,210
Direct labour rate variance	210 (A)

1,000 units should have used	4,000 hrs
but did use	4,200 hrs
Variance in hours	200 hrs (A)
× standard rate per hour	× £5
Direct labour efficiency variance	£1,000 (A)

Variable overhead total variance

The difference between what the output should have cost and what it did cost, in terms of variable overhead

Variable overhead expenditure variance

The difference between the actual variable overhead incurred and the amount that should have been incurred in the hours actively worked

Variable overhead efficiency variance

The difference between the standard cost of the hours that should have been worked and the standard cost of the hours that were worked

Example

	£
1,000 units should have cost (× £8)	8,000
but did cost	9,450
Variable o/hd total variance	1,450 (A)

	£
4,200 hrs should have cost (× £2)	8,400
but did cost	9,450
Variable o/hd exp'd variance	1,050 (A)

Labour efficiency variance in hrs	200 hrs (A)
× standard rate per hour	× £2
Variable o/hd efficiency variance	£400 (A)

The **total variance** is the difference between fixed overhead incurred and fixed overhead absorbed (= under- or over-absorbed fixed overhead).

Expenditure variance

The difference between budgeted and actual fixed overhead expenditure

Example

	£
Budgeted o/hd (1,200 × £24)	28,800
Actual overhead	25,000
Expenditure variance	**3,800** (F)

Causes of under/over absorption

- Actual expenditure ≠ budgeted expenditure ⟹ expenditure variance
- Actual prod'n (units or hrs) ≠ budgeted prod'n ⟹ volume variance

Example

	£
Overhead incurred	25,000
Overhead absorbed (1,000 × £24)	24,000
Under-absorbed overhead/total variance	1,000 (A)*

Volume variance

The difference between actual and budgeted production units × standard absorption rate per unit

Example

	£
Actual prod'n at std rate (1,000 × £24)	24,000
Budgeted prod'n at std rate (1,200 × £24)	28,800
Volume variance	**4,800** (A)*

*(A) because actual output less than budgeted output

Efficiency variance

Shows how much of the under/over absorption is due to efficiency of labour/plant

The difference between the number of hours that production should have taken and the number of hours worked × standard absorption rate per hour

Example

Labour efficiency variance in hrs	200 hrs (A)
× standard rate per hr	× £6
Efficiency variance	**£1,200** (A)

This is usually the labour efficiency variance in hours and so is also similar to the variable overhead efficiency variance.

Note the variance is (A) when actual hours are less than budgeted hours.

Capacity variance

Shows how much of the under/over absorption is due to hours worked being more or less than budgeted

The difference between budgeted hours of work and actual hours worked × standard absorption rate per hour

Example

Budgeted hours (1,200 × 4)	4,800 hrs
Actual hours	4,200 hrs
Variance in hrs	600 hrs(A)
× std rate per hr	× £6
Capacity variance	**£3,600** (A)

In a marginal costing system there is no volume variance.

The total fixed overhead variance is the difference between the overhead incurred and the overhead absorbed into the cost of production (= under- or over-absorbed overhead). There are two reasons why under or over absorption occur.

Budgeted expenditure ≠ actual expenditure

Expenditure variance
Fixed overhead not absorbed into the cost of production but charged to the P&L account because of a difference between budgeted and actual expenditures

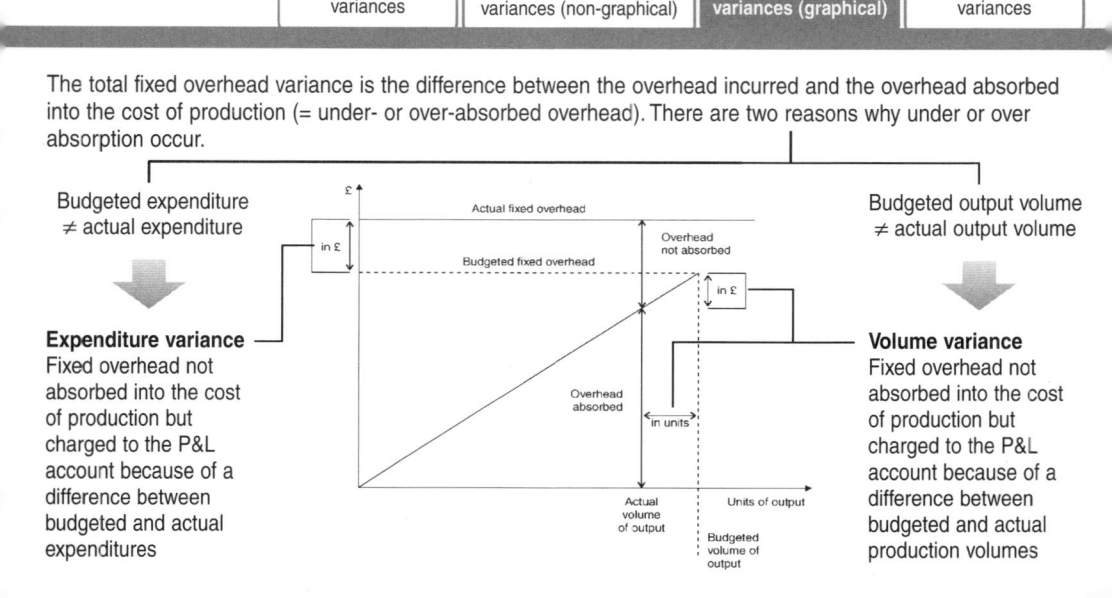

Budgeted output volume ≠ actual output volume

Volume variance
Fixed overhead not absorbed into the cost of production but charged to the P&L account because of a difference between budgeted and actual production volumes

There are two reasons for a difference between budgeted and actual production volumes (➡ volume variance).

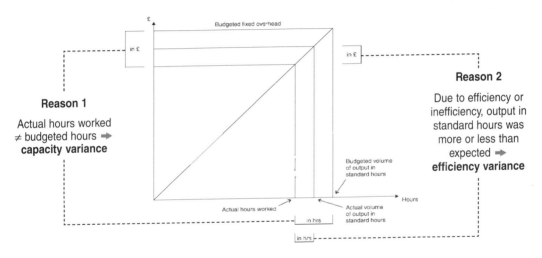

Reason 1

Actual hours worked ≠ budgeted hours ➡ **capacity variance**

Reason 2

Due to efficiency or inefficiency, output in standard hours was more or less than expected ➡ **efficiency variance**

2: Variance analysis

Selling (or sales) price variance

A measure of the effect on expected profit of a different selling price to standard

The difference between what the sales revenue should have been for the actual quantity sold, and what it was

Example

```
                                    £
Revenue from 900 units should
have been (× £150)               135,000
but was (× £140)                 126,000
                                 ───────
Selling price variance             9,000 (A)
```

Don't forget to value the sales volume variance at standard contribution margin if marginal costing is in use.

The interdependence between the two variances should be clear.

Sales volume variance

A measure of the effect on expected profit of a different sales volume to that budgeted

The difference between the actual units sold and the budgeted quantity, valued at the standard profit per unit

Example

```
Budgeted sales volume           1,000 units
Actual sales volume               900 units
                                ───────────
Variance in units                 100 units (A)
× std profit per unit
(× £(150 − 102))
× £48
                                ───────────
Sales volume variance          £4,800 (A)
```

3: Further variance analysis

Topic List

Operating statements

Working backwards

Materials mix and yield variances

Labour mix and yield variances

With all variance calculations, from the most basic (such as the calculation of variable cost variances) to the more complex mix and yield variances summarised in this chapter, it is vital you do not simply learn formulae. You must understand what your calculations are supposed to show. You therefore need to be completely happy with the basic variances in Chapter 2 before you work through this chapter.

> Key questions to try in the kit: 12,16
> Refer to MCQ cards (with Ch 4): 28-37

Most common presentation (absorption costing)

	£	£
Budgeted profit		X
Sales variances – price	X	
– volume	X	
		X
Actual sales minus standard cost of sales		X

Cost variances	£ (F)	£ (A)	
Material price etc	X		
Fixed o/hd volume etc		X	
	X	X	X
Actual profit			X

Most common presentation (marginal costing)

	£	£
Budgeted profit		X
Budgeted fixed production overhead		X
Budgeted contribution		X
Sales variances (price and volume)		X
Actual sales minus std variable cost of sales		X
Variable cost variances		X
Actual contribution		X
Budgeted fixed production overhead	X	
Expenditure variance	X	
Actual fixed production overhead		X
Actual profit		X

Stock adjustment

If actual sales volume ≠ actual production volume, and stock is valued at actual cost, the difference between closing stock valuations at actual cost and standard cost is added to the bottom of the operating statement.

One way that the examiner can test your understanding of variance analysis is to provide information about variances from which you have to 'work backwards' to determine the actual results. You need to take an algebraic approach as shown in the examples.

This type of question really tests your understanding of the subject. If you simply memorise variance formulae you will have difficulty in answering such questions.

Example

Suppose we do not know the actual hours.

Total direct wages cost	£21,210
Less rate variance (given)	£210 (A)
Standard rate for actual hrs	£21,000
÷ standard rate per hr (given)	÷ £5
Actual hours worked	4,200 hrs

Example

Suppose we do not know the actual material used.

Let the number of kgs purchased and used = x

	£
x kgs should have cost (× £10)	10.0x
but did cost (× £9.50)	9.5x
Material price variance	0.5x (F)

Having been provided with the variance (£2,425 (F)), you can calculate x = 2,425/0.5 = 4,850 kgs.

If a product requires two or more raw materials, and the proportions of the materials are changeable and controllable, the materials usage variance can be split into a mix of a mix variance and a yield variance.

Materials yield variance

- A measure of the effect on costs of inputs yielding more or less than expected
- Calculated as the difference between the expected output and the actual output, valued at the standard cost per unit of output

Calculating the yield variance

1 Find, for one unit of output, the standard *total* materials usage in kgs, litres etc, and the cost of this standard usage.

2 Determine the standard output from the actual total quantity input.

Example

1 Std input to produce 1 unit of X:

A	20 kgs × £10	£200
B	30 kgs × £5	£150
	50 kgs	£350

In May, 13 units of X were produced from 250kg of A and 350 kgs of B.

2 (250+350)kgs should have

yielded (÷ 50kgs)	12X
but did yield	13X
Yield variance in units	1X (F)
× standard cost per unit of output	× £350
Yield variance in £	£350 (F)

Materials mix variance

- A measure of whether the actual mix is cheaper or more expensive than the standard

- Calculated as the difference between the actual total quantity used in the standard mix and the actual quantity used in the actual mix, **valued** using one of two methods

  EITHER   Standard input price of each material

  OR   The difference between the standard weighted average price and the individual standard input prices

Calculating the mix variance

1 Find the standard proportions of the mix.

2 Calculate the standard mix of the actual materials used.

3 Find (in kgs, litres etc for each input) the differences between what should have been used and what was used.

4 Value the variances using one of the two methods.

You are only required to be able to calculate total mix variances. It therefore does not matter which of the valuation methods you use as the total variance is the same using both approaches. We recommend using the standard input price as it is slightly quicker.

Example (cont'd from page 20)

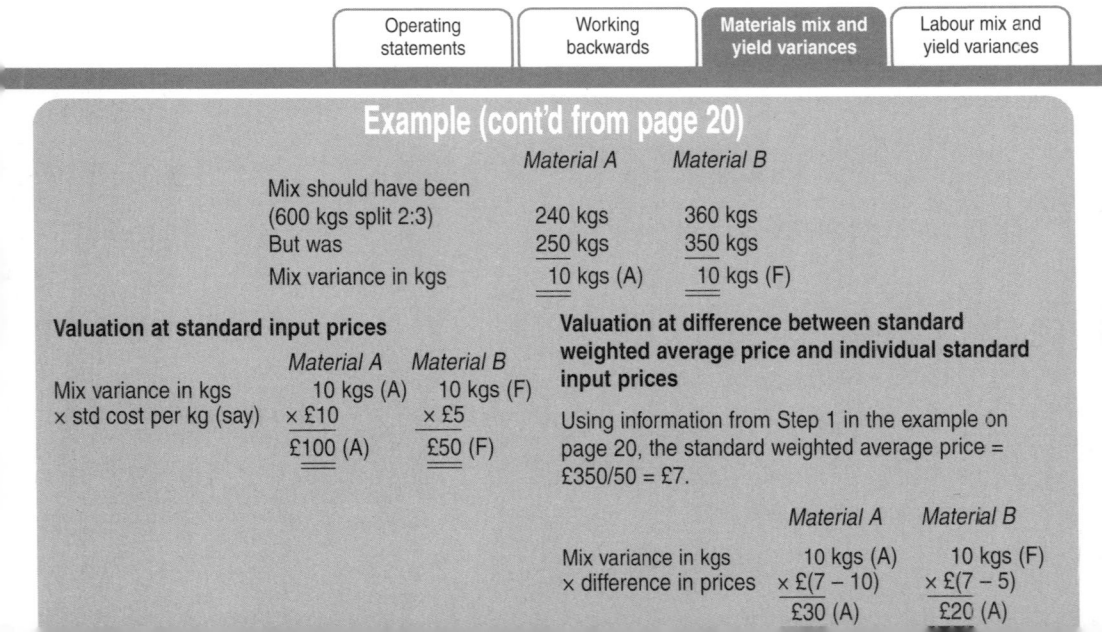

	Material A	*Material B*
Mix should have been (600 kgs split 2:3)	240 kgs	360 kgs
But was	250 kgs	350 kgs
Mix variance in kgs	10 kgs (A)	10 kgs (F)

Valuation at standard input prices

	Material A	*Material B*
Mix variance in kgs	10 kgs (A)	10 kgs (F)
× std cost per kg (say)	× £10	× £5
	£100 (A)	£50 (F)

Valuation at difference between standard weighted average price and individual standard input prices

Using information from Step 1 in the example on page 20, the standard weighted average price = £350/50 = £7.

	Material A	*Material B*
Mix variance in kgs	10 kgs (A)	10 kgs (F)
× difference in prices	× £(7 − 10)	× £(7 − 5)
	£30 (A)	£20 (A)

The total mix variance in quantity (here 10 kgs (A) + 10 kgs (F)) is always zero.

The total mix variance (in £) is the same by both methods, but the individual mix variances are different.

The overall mix variance (in £) is adverse because more of the more expensive material was used than anticipated.

Actual input of material compared with standard	Standard input price compared with weighted average price	Variance
More (A)	Greater	(A)
More (A)	Less	(F)
Less (F)	Greater	(F)
Less (F)	Less	(A)

Now that only total mix variances are examinable, look out for them in particular in Section A of the paper.

Labour mix variance

- Also known as the **team composition variance**

- A measure of whether the actual mix of labour grades is cheaper or more expensive than the standard mix

- Calculated in exactly the same way as the materials mix variance

As with the materials mix variance, CIMA recommends two methods of valuing the labour mix variance.

Labour yield variance

- Also known as the **team productivity variance**
- Shows how productively people are working
- Calculated in exactly the same way as the materials yield variance

Example

Standard hours for actual mix: 85 hours of grade A labour

Actual hours: 90 hours of grade A labour

Weighted average rate per hour: £15
Standard rate per hour for grade A labour: £13

Using the weighted average method, the mix variance for grade A labour is favourable because more hours than standard were worked at a standard rate less than the weighted average rate.

Using the standard input rate method, however, the mix variance for grade A labour would be adverse because more hours than standard were worked.

Topic List

Variance interpretation

Variance investigation

Variance investigation models

Joint variances

Benchmarking

'Interpretation of variances: interrelationship, significance' is a specific syllabus topic. You are likely to be required to perform calculations of variances and to analyse and explain your results.

Key questions to try in the kit: 1,2,19
Refer to MCQ cards (with Ch 3): 28-37

Variance	Favourable	Adverse
Material price	Unforeseen discounts received, greater care in purchasing	Price increase (inflation, seasonal variations, rush orders), careless purchasing
Material usage	Higher quality material, more effective use of material	Defective material, excessive waste, theft, stricter quality control
Labour rate	Use of workers with a lower rate of pay than standard	Unexpected overtime working (premium rate), productivity bonuses, rate increase
Idle time	Could occur if there is budgeted idle time	Machine breakdown, non-availability of material, illness or injury to worker

Labour efficiency	Output produced more quickly than expected due to worker motivation, better quality equipment/materials	Lost time/down time/rest periods in excess of standard allowed, poor labour productivity due to lack of training, sub-standard materials, shorter batch runs
Overhead expenditure	Either the price component (eg salaries) or usage component (eg number of staff) can vary.	
Overhead efficiency	Production or level of activity greater/less than budgeted due to labour efficiency/inefficiency.	
Overhead capacity	Actual time worked greater than budgeted (eg overtime)	Excessive idle time, shortage of plant capacity, strikes

Do not learn these causes by rote. You must be able to apply them to the scenario of the question.

In general, when deciding whether or not to investigate a particular variance, bear in mind six points.

- Materiality
- Controllability
- Variance trend —— Consider using % variance charts
- Costs v benefits
- Type of performance standard used
- Interdependence/interrelationship

Why might variances occur?

- Actual outcome measurement errors
- Out of date standards
- Inefficient or efficient operations
- Random or chance fluctuations (remember that standards are average)

The cause of one (adverse) variance may be wholly or partially explained by the cause of another (favourable) variance.

- Material price and usage variances
- Material price and labour efficiency variances
- Labour rate and efficiency variances
- Labour rate and material usage variances
- Sales price and volume variances
- Materials mix and yield variances

The significance of a variance can be assessed using a variance investigation model.

Rule-of-thumb method

This involves deciding a limit, say 5%, and if a variance is within 5% of standard in any one period, it should be considered immaterial. Only if it exceeds the limit should it be considered materially significant and worthy of investigation.

Problems
■ Ignores trend in and past history of variances
■ Ignores costs/benefits
■ Ignores absolute materiality
■ Ignores sharp fluctuations within the limit set
■ Deciding on pre-set percentage
■ How to treat favourable and adverse variances

Some difficulties can be overcome by varying the pre-set percentage from account to account.

Statistical significance model

Historical data is used to calculate an expected average and the standard deviation of variation around this average when the process is under control (ie when variances are simply due to random fluctuations), on the assumption that the variances are normally distributed.

A variance will be investigated if it is more than an amount that the estimated normal distribution suggests is likely if the process is in control.

Advantages

■ Important costs that normally vary by only a small amount from standard will be signalled for investigation if variances increase significantly.

■ Costs that usually fluctuate by large amounts will not be signalled for investigation unless variances are extremely large.

The main disadvantage is the problem of assessing standard deviations.

Example

A variance greater than 1.96 standard deviations from the mean has only a 2½% chance of happening under normal operating conditions. This is unusual and so such a variance should be investigated.

Statistical control charts

$\bar{x}$ control chart

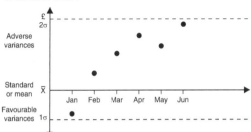

- Limits are set at a certain number of standard deviations depending on the level of confidence required
- Highlights trends
- Identifies variances of such magnitude that they are unlikely to have arisen by chance

Cusum chart

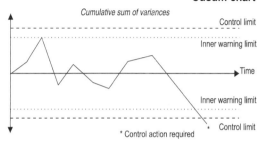

- Shows cumulative sum of variances
- Trends detected earlier than when using $\bar{x}$ control chart

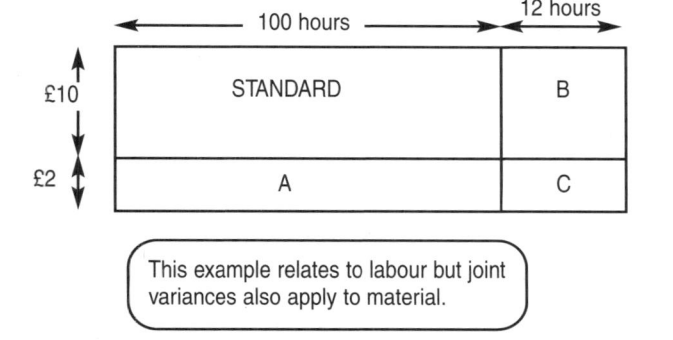

- Traditional rate variance = A + C
- Traditional efficiency variance = B
- Joint variance = C
  - The manager responsible for labour rates should be responsible for A + 2C because he/she could have paid £10 instead of £12 for the hours worked
  - The production manager should be responsible for B + C because some of the rate variance (on the extra hours over standard) could have been avoided by him/her

This example relates to labour but joint variances also apply to material.

The excess wage rate of the excess hours worked could have been avoided by either of the two managers. In other words the joint variance should be reported to each of the managers jointly responsible for it.

'The establishment, through data gathering, of targets and comparators, through whose use relative levels of performance (and particularly areas of under-performance) can be identified. By the adoption of identified best practices it is hoped that performance will improve.' (CIMA)

Like standard costing, benchmarking is a comparison exercise through which an organisation attempts to improve performance.

Types of benchmarking

- **Internal** Comparing the performance of one operating unit or function with another in the same industry

- **Functional/operational/generic** Comparing performance of an internal function with the best external practitioners of the function, regardless of the industry

- **Competitive** Comparing performance with direct competitors (using, for example, reverse engineering)

- **Strategic** Type of competitive benchmarking aimed at strategic action and organisational change

Obtaining information

- Financial information about competitors is easier to acquire than non-financial information.

- Information about products can be obtained from reverse engineering, product literature, media comment and trade associations.

- Information about processes is more difficult to find. Such information can be obtained from group companies or non-competing organisations in the same industry.

Advantages include

- An effective method of implementing change

- Flexible (can be used in private and public sectors and by staff at different levels of responsibility)

- Cross comparisons are more likely to expose radical new ways of doing things

- Establishes a desire for continuous improvement

Benchmarking and standards

Benchmarking allows attainable standards to be set. ➡ These can be regularly reviewed in the light of benchmarking information. ➡ They then become part of a programme of continuous improvement by becoming increasingly demanding.

5: Budgets

Topic List

Budgetary planning and control

Budget preparation

Cash budgets

Alternative approaches

Budgeting with uncertainty

*You must be able to prepare budgets (functional, cash and master) from information provided **and** be able to recommend appropriate management action given the position shown by the budget you prepare.*

The budgeting systems examined towards the end of this chapter may be more appropriate for certain organisations and/or for certain types of cost and revenue than the traditional system considered at the beginning of it.

Key questions to try in the kit: 21,22,29
Refer to MCQ cards: 38-57

Objectives of a budgetary planning and control system

- Ensure the organisation's objectives are achieved
- Compel planning
- Communicate ideas and plans
- Co-ordinate activities
- Provide a framework for responsibility accounting
- Establish a system of control
- Motivate employees to improve their performance

You need to be able to explain why organisations prepare plans. Planning forces management to look ahead, to set out detailed plans for achieving the targets for each department, operation and (ideally) each manager, and to anticipate problems. It therefore prevents managers from relying on ad-hoc or uncoordinated planning which may be detrimental to the performance of the organisation.

Planning

The overall planning process covers both the long term and the short term.

Types of planning

- **Strategic / corporate / long-range planning** (selecting strategies to attain objectives)

- **Budgetary / short-term tactical planning** (preparing detailed plans covering one year)

- **Operation planning** (planning on a day-to-day basis how resources will be used)

1. Communication of details of the budget policy and guidelines
2. Identification of **principal/key/limiting budget factor** (usually sales)
3. Preparation of a **sales budget** based on a sales forecast (assuming sales is key budget factor)
4. Preparation of a **finished goods stock budget** (to determine the planned change in finished stock levels)
5. Preparation of a **production budget** (sales ± budgeted change in finished goods stock, in units)
6. Preparation of **budgets for production resources** (labour, material usage etc)
7. Preparation of a **raw materials stock budget** (to determine the planned change in raw materials stock levels)
8. Preparation of a **raw materials purchases budget** (usage ± budgeted change in raw materials stock, taking account of discounts)
9. Preparation of **overhead costs budgets**
10. Calculation of OARs (if absorption costing is used)
11. Preparation of **cash budget** (and capital expenditure, working capital budgets etc)
12. Negotiation of budgets with superiors
13. Co-ordination and final acceptance of the budgets
14. Production of a **master budget** (budgeted P&L a/c, budgeted balance sheet, cash budget)
15. Budget review (to ensure budgets are compatible/to incorporate changes in organisational policies)

Standard hours

If you are asked to prepare the labour budget for the production of a number of dissimilar units, you can convert the budgeted output into standard hours of production and construct a labour budget accordingly.

Appropriate action

You must be able to recommend action given the information shown in budgets prepared.

If a budget indicates a shortfall in labour hours, you could suggest overtime working, reduction in wastage, or improvement in productivity.

If a budget indicates that capacity will exceed sales demand for a length of time, consideration should be given to product diversification, a reduction in selling price (if demand is elastic) and so on. A shortfall in capacity might require overtime, subcontracting, machine hire or new sources of materials.

Stock control formulae

In an exam you may be required to use stock control formulae to determine stock levels.

- **Reorder level** = maximum usage × maximum lead time

- $EOQ = \sqrt{\dfrac{2CoD}{Ch}}$

- **Minimum level** = reorder level − (average usage × average lead time)

- **Maximum level** = reorder level + reorder quantity − (minimum usage × minimum lead time)

Steps in the preparation of a cash budget

1   Set up a proforma.

2   Establish budgeted sales month by month. Bearing in mind the credit period taken by debtors and taking discounts into account, calculate when budgeted sales revenue will be received as cash and when opening debtors will pay.

3   Establish when any other cash income will be received.

4   Establish, for each month, production quantities and hence materials usage quantities, materials stock changes and the quantity and cost of materials purchases. Bearing in mind the credit period taken, calculate when cash payments to suppliers will be made and when the amount due to opening creditors will be paid.

5   Establish when any other cash payments (excluding non-cash items such as depreciation) will be paid.

> **Include at the foot of every column of your cash budget the opening cash position, the net cash flow and the closing cash position.**

Usefulness

The cash budget shows the cash position as a result of all plans made during the budgetary process and so gives management the opportunity to take appropriate control action.

Appropriate control action

- **Short-term surplus.** Pay creditors early to obtain discount or make short-term investments
- **Short-term deficit.** Increase creditors, reduce debtors, arrange an overdraft
- **Long-term surplus.** Expand, diversify, replace/update fixed assets
- **Long-term deficit.** Issue share capital, consider shutdown/divestment opportunities

Cash flow versus profit

These are likely to be different.

- Not all cash receipts affect P&L a/c income (eg issue of new shares)
- Not all cash payments affect P&L a/c expenditure (eg purchase of fixed assets)
- Some items in the P&L a/c are not cash flows (eg depreciation)
- Timings of cash receipts and payments may not coincide with P&L a/c recording (eg declaration and payment of dividend)

Bad debts will never be recovered in cash and doubtful debts may not be received, so adjust if necessary for such items.

Incremental budgeting

This involves adding a certain percentage to last year's budget to allow for growth and inflation. It encourages slack and wasteful spending to creep into budgets.

contrast with

ZBB

This approach treats the preparation of the budget for each period as an independent planning exercise: the initial budget is zero and every item of expenditure has to be justified in its entirety to be included.

Three-step approach to ZBB

1 Define **decision packages** (description of a specific activity so that it can be evaluated and ranked).

2 Evaluate and rank packages on the basis of their benefit to the organisation.

3 Allocate resources according to the funds available and the ranking of packages.

Mutually exclusive packages

Incremental packages

Advantages of ZBB

☑ Identifies and removes inefficient and/or obsolete operations

☑ Forces employees to avoid wasteful expenditure

☑ Leads to a more efficient allocation of resources

☑ Challenges the status quo

Disadvantages of ZBB

☒ Involves time and effort

☒ Can cause suspicion when introduced

☒ Costs and benefits of different alternative courses of action can be difficult to quantity

☒ Ranking can prove problematic

☒ Short term v long term trade-off

Applications of ZBB

- Support expenses
- Service industries
- Not-for-profit organisations
- Discretionary costs
- Rationalisation measures

Programme planning and budgeting systems (PPBS)

PPBS set a budget in terms of programmes (groups of activities with common objectives). By focusing on objectives, the budget is orientated towards the ultimate output of the organisation (which contrasts with the traditional approach to budgeting, which focuses on inputs (labour, material, etc)).

Particular uses of PPBS

- Public sector
- Non-profit seeking organisations

PPBS ensures expenditure is focused on the programmes/ activities that generate the most beneficial results and is in line with public demands for **accountability**.

> **Disadvantages of traditional budgeting for non-profit seeking organisations**
>
> - Activities span several years, but the emphasis is on annual figures.
>
> - It is difficult to incorporate the mainly non-financial planned/actual achievements.
>
> - Costs for a particular objective are spread across a number of cost categories.
>
> - There is no evidence of how effectively/ efficiently resources are used.

Discretionary costs

Costs of a process for which there is no clear relationship between its input and its output, often because the output is difficult to measure, in terms of quantity and/or quality

Control of discretionary costs

Control (perhaps minimum standards of performance) is problematic because some measure of output is required. Inputs can be controlled, however, if the budget acts as a device to ensure financial resources allocated to the activity are not exceeded.

Budgeting for discretionary costs

This can be made easier by converting them into engineered costs.

- Develop suitable output measures
- Understand how input impacts on output

ABC might be useful.

If a discretionary cost cannot be converted into an engineered cost, ZBB or PPBS will be needed.

It is obviously much easier to budget for direct material cost (an engineered cost) than for the cost of the accounts department (discretionary cost).

Rolling/continuous budgets

Instead of preparing a periodic budget annually for the full budget period, this process involves the preparation of budgets every one, two, three or four months. Each budget covers the next 12 months so that the current budget is extended by an extra period as the current period ends.

If a rolling budget is prepared every three months, the first three months of the period would be planned in great detail and the remaining nine months in less detail because of increased uncertainty about the longer-term future.

Advantages of rolling budgets

- ☑ They reduce uncertainty.
- ☑ An up-to-date budget is always available.
- ☑ Realistic budgets are better motivators.
- ☑ Inflation and major changes in market conditions can be incorporated more accurately into the budget.

Disadvantages of rolling budgets

- ☒ They involve more time, effort and money.
- ☒ Managers can doubt the value of preparing one budget after another.
- ☒ They could involve revisions to standard costs and hence stock valuations.

It might actually be simpler to update the annual budget once or twice during the year.

5: Budgets

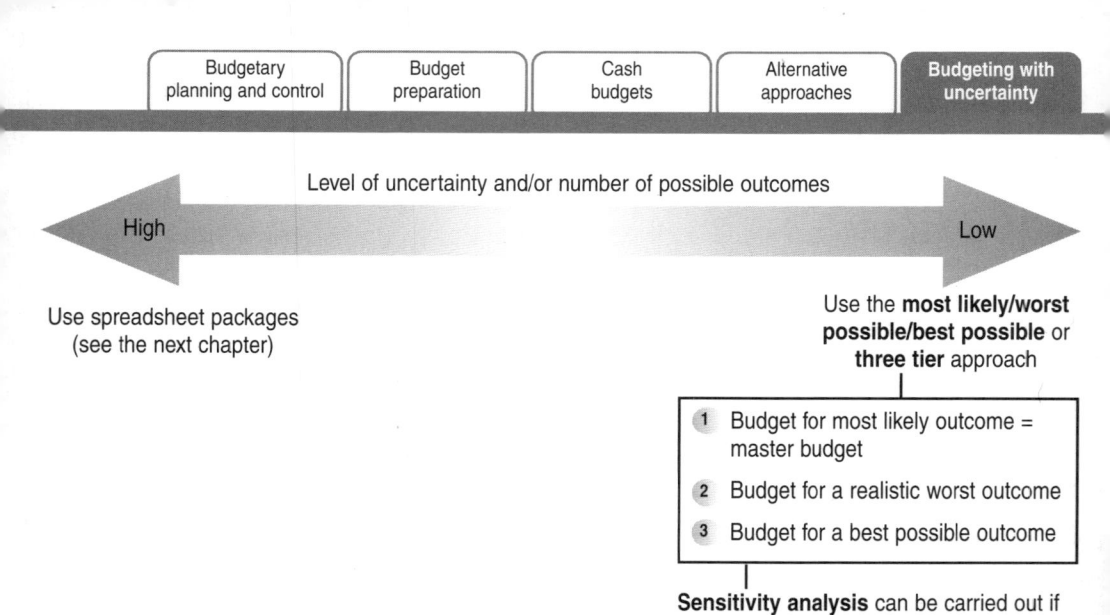

Budgetary planning and control | Budget preparation | Cash budgets | Alternative approaches | **Budgeting with uncertainty**

Level of uncertainty and/or number of possible outcomes

High

Low

Use spreadsheet packages (see the next chapter)

Use the **most likely/worst possible/best possible** or **three tier** approach

1. Budget for most likely outcome = master budget

2. Budget for a realistic worst outcome

3. Budget for a best possible outcome

Sensitivity analysis can be carried out if this information is presented graphically.

6: Forecasting

The techniques summarised in this chapter aim to produce forecasts (estimates of what might happen in the future). A budget, on the other hand, is a plan of what the organisation is aiming to achieve and what it has set as a target.

Key questions to try in the kit: 30,31
Refer to MCQ cards: 58-70

Linear regression analysis (least squares technique) finds the equation of the straight line **(line of best fit)** which has the general form **Y = a +bX**

where **Y = dependent variable = total cost**
 X = independent variable = level of activity
 a = intercept of line on y axis = fixed cost
 b = gradient of line = variable cost per unit

Historical data (adjusted for inflation) provide readings for x and y. These readings are then substituted into formulae for a and b.

$$b = \frac{n\Sigma XY - \Sigma X \Sigma Y}{n\Sigma X^2 - (\Sigma X)^2} \quad \text{and} \quad a = \frac{\Sigma Y}{n} - \frac{b\Sigma X}{n}$$

where n = number of pairs of data for X and Y.

> **The formulae for a and b will be provided in the exam.**

Conditions necessary for the use of linear regression analysis

- A linear cost function is assumed.
- Historical cost data is accurately recorded.
- There are 10+ pairs of data.
- The activity levels in the historical data cover the full normal range of activity.
- Data is adjusted to account for inflation.
- Past conditions are indicative of future conditions.
- The value of Y can be predicted from the value of X.

Regression analysis and forecasting

Forecasting costs

Once the equation has been determined, a value for X (activity level) can be substituted into the equation and a value for Y (total cost at that activity level) forecast.

Example

Calculations produce $Y = 17 + 3.6X$ (where X is in '000 units and Y is in £'000). Fixed costs are therefore £17,000 and variable cost per unit is £3,600.

Predicted cost (Y) if activity level (X) is 13,000 units = $17 + (3.6 \times 13) = 63.8 = £63,800$

Forecasting sales

1. Calculate a regression line (trend line) $Y = a + bX$, where Y = sales and X = period of time.

2. Years (days/months) become the X variable in the regression formulae by numbering them from 1 upwards.

3. A forecast (Y) for a particular time period (X) is determined by substitution of the value for X into the trend line equation.

Example

Year	X	Sales (Y) '000 units
20X0	1	21 ⎤
20X1	2	23 ⎥ extract
20X2	3	26 ⎦

Calculations produce $Y = 18 + 2.7X$

Predicted sales (Y) in 20X6 (X = 7)
$$= 18 + (2.7 \times 7)$$
$$= 36.9$$
$$= £36,900 \text{ units}$$

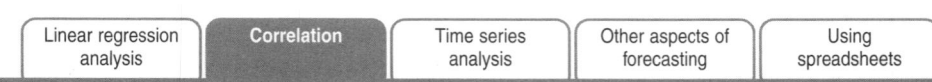

| Linear regression analysis | **Correlation** | Time series analysis | Other aspects of forecasting | Using spreadsheets |

Correlation

> The extent to which the value of a dependent variable is related to the value of an independent variable

Coefficient of correlation, r

- Also known as the **Pearsonian coefficient of correlation** or the **product moment correlation coefficient**, this measures the degree of correlation.

- $r = \dfrac{n\sum XY - \sum X \sum Y}{\sqrt{(n\sum X^2 - (\sum X)^2)(n\sum Y^2 - (\sum Y)^2)}}$

- r has a value between −1 (perfect negative correlation) and +1 (perfect positive correlation)

Degrees of correlation

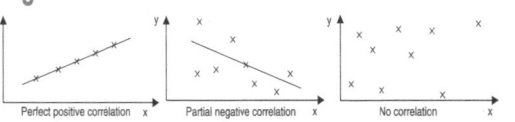

Perfect negative correlation and partial positive correlation are also possible.

Coefficient of determination, r^2

- This indicates the change in Y that can be predicted by a change in X.

- If $r^2 = 0.95$, 95% of the variation in the value of Y can be predicted from variations in X.

- The closer r^2 is to 1, the greater the degree of confidence that X (level of activity) can be used to predict accurately Y (cost).

Finding the trend (T)

1. The trend line can be drawn **by eye** on a graph as a line of best fit.

2. **Linear regression analysis** (see page 50)

3. **Moving averages** ⟶

Of an even number of periods

Year	Sales	Moving total of 4 yrs' sales	Moving average of 4 yrs' sales	Mid-point of 2 moving av'ges TREND
20X1	600			
20X2	840			
		2,580*	645.0	
20X3	420			650.00
		2,620**	655.0	
20X4	720			
20X5	640			

*(600+840+420+720)   **(840+420+720+640)

Of an odd number of periods

Year	Sales	Moving total of 3 yrs' sales	Moving av. of 3 yrs' sales (÷3) TREND
20X0	390		
20X1	380	1,230	410
20X2	460	1,290	430
20X3	450		

Finding the seasonal variations (S)

1 Calculate the seasonal variations

- **Additive model** (Y = T + S)
  S = actual – trend (S = Y – T)

- **Multiplicative/proportional model**
  (Y = T × S)
  S = actual ÷ trend (S = Y/T)

			Seasonal variation	
Wk 1	Actual	Trend	Add model	Prop model
M	80	92.70	–12.70	0.863
T	104	93.12	+10.88	1.117

2 Take an average of the variations

The November 2001 exam question on this topic did not require you to do this averaging as, very conveniently, the seasonal variations were the same in each year.

	Additive model		Proportional model	
	M	T	M	T
Wk 1	–12.70	+10.88	0.863	1.117
Wk 2	–12.80	+14.78	0.865	1.155
Total	–25.50	+25.66	1.728	2.272
Average	–12.75	+12.83	0.864	1.136

3 Adjust the total of the variations

Additive model: to zero	Mon	Tues	Wed	Thurs	Fri	Total
Average	−12.75	+12.83	+0.91	+27.49	−32.43	−3.95
Adjustment (3.95/5)	+0.79	+0.79	+0.79	+0.79	+0.79	+3.95
Final estimate	−11.96	13.62	1.70	28.28	−31.64	0.00
Round to	−12	14	2	28	−32	

Proportional model: to number of items in cycle	Mon	Tues	Wed	Thurs	Fri	Total
Average	0.8640	1.1360	1.0095	1.2890	0.6600	4.9585
Adjustment (5 − 4.9585)/5	0.0083	0.0083	0.0083	0.0083	0.0083	0.0415
Final estimate	0.8723	1.1443	1.0178	1.2973	0.6683	5.0000
Round to	0.87	1.14	1.02	1.3	0.67	

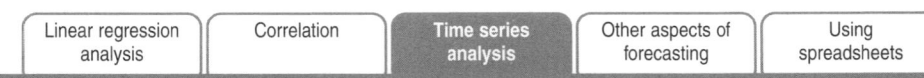

Time series analysis and forecasting

Calculate a trend line and then use the trend line to forecast future values and adjust these values by the applicable seasonal variation.

- **Using inspection** (extend the line of best fit)
- **Linear regression analysis** (the sales forecast (Y) for a particular time period (X) is determined by substituting the value for X into the trend line equation – see page 49)
- **Common sense**

Example

1

	Trend values (quarter)			
Year	1st	2nd	3rd	4th
1			18.75	19.375
2	20	20.5	21	21.5
3	22.125	22.75		

2 Average seasonal variations for quarters 1 to 4 are –0.1, +12.4, +1.1 and –13.4 respectively.

3 The trend line indicates an increase of about 0.6 per quarter, which can be checked as follows.

$$\frac{22.75\,(Yr3Q_2) - 18.75\,(Yr1Q_3)}{7\,(Number\ of\ Qs)} = 0.57 \approx 0.6$$

4 Trend line forecast for year 4 quarter 1 is as follows.

YearQ					Trend line
3	2nd	actual trend	22.75, say		22.8
	3rd	forecast trend	= 22.8 + 0.6	=	23.4
	4th	forecast trend	= 23.4 + 0.6	=	24.0
4	1st	forecast trend	= 24.0 + 0.6	=	24.6

5 Final forecast = 24.6 – 0.1 (seasonal variation) = 24.5

6 If the multiplicative model variation for quarter 1 was 0.98, year 4 quarter 1 prediction = 24.6 × 0.98 = 24.1

Forecasting with scatter diagrams

1. Plot cost and activity data on a graph.
2. Draw a 'line of best fit' through the middle of the plotted points.
3. Fixed costs = intercept on vertical axis
4. Variable cost per unit = (total cost (read from the graph) – fixed cost) ÷ activity level

Forecasting problems

- Political, economic, environmental, technological and social changes make forecasting difficult.
- The further into the future the forecast, the more unreliable it is.
- The less data available for the forecast, the less reliable it is.
- The pattern of trend and seasonal variations may not continue.

Factors to consider when forecasting sales

- Past sales patterns
- New technology
- Market research results
- Changing consumer tastes
- Legislation
- Economic environment
- Anticipated advertising
- Pricing policies and discounts offered
- Environment
- Competition
- Available mathematical techniques

Sensitivity analysis

Once a model has been constructed, consequences of changes in any of the variables may be tested by asking **'what if'** questions (eg 'What if sales in 20X3 were 2,000 units instead of 2,200 units?'), a form of sensitivity analysis.

Spreadsheet modelling

Spreadsheet packages can be used to build business models to assist the forecasting and planning process.

1   **Insert text** to identify what data goes into each row and each column.
2   **Specify how the numerical data in the model should be derived.**
    ■ Keyboard input
    ■ Calculation from other data in the model
    ■ Retrieved from data on a disk file

The methods used to make a forecast/estimate should be in keeping with the nature, quantity and reliability of the data on which the forecast/estimate will be based. There is little point in using a 'sophisticated' technique with unreliable data; on the other hand, if there is a lot of accurate data about historical costs, use of the scatter diagram method to estimate costs would be a waste of the data.

Analysing relationships

The relationship between dependent/ independent variables might be **curvilinear** **($Y = aX^b$)**. Nowadays spreadsheet packages can be used to carry out a series of repetitive calculations to determine a and b and the resulting equation can be used for forecasting.

7: Budgets – control and performance measurement

Topic List

Behavioural aspects

Balanced scorecard

Budgetary control

Feedback and feedforward control

Controllable/uncontrollable costs

Keep an open mind when revising about and answering questions on the behavioural aspects of budgeting as there are no ideal solutions to the conflict caused by the operation of a budgetary control system.

Key questions to try in the kit: 36,38,39,45
Refer to MCQ cards: 71-91

Budgets as a source of conflict

Budgeting is a multi-purpose activity (see Chapter 6) and so it means different things to different people.

- A forecast
- A means of allocating resources
- A yardstick
- A target

Conflict is therefore inevitable.

Negative effects of budgets include

- **At the planning stage**
  - Managers may fail to co-ordinate plans with those of other budget centres.
  - They may build slack into expenditure estimates.

- **When putting plans into action**
  - There could be minimal co-operation and communication between managers.
  - Managers might try to achieve targets but not beat them.

- **Using control information**
  - Resentment could occur, managers seeing the information as part of a system of trying to find fault with their work.
  - Scepticism of the value of information if it is inaccurate, too late or not understood could arise.

Participation

Budget-setting styles

- Imposed (from the top down)
- Participative (from the bottom up)
- Negotiated

Advantages of participative approach include

- ☑ More realistic budgets
- ☑ Co-ordination, morale and motivation improved
- ☑ Increased management commitment to objectives

Disadvantages of participative approach include

- ☒ More time-consuming
- ☒ Budgetary slack may be introduced
- ☒ Can support 'empire building'

Performance evaluation

An important source of motivation to perform well (to achieve budget targets, to eliminate adverse variances) is being kept informed about how actual results are progressing compared with target.

Ways of using budgetary information to evaluate performance

- Budget-constrained style
- Profit-conscious style
- Non-accounting style

Despite conventional assumptions, research suggests accounting performance measures lead to a lack of goal congruence.

7: Budgets – control and performance measurement

Budgets as targets

Can budgets, as targets, motivate managers to achieve a high level of performance?

- *Ideal standards* are demotivating because adverse efficiency variances are always reported.

- *Low standards* are demotivating because there is no sense of achievement in attainment, no impetus to try harder.

- *Normal levels* of attainment encourage budgetary slack.

To ensure managers are properly motivated, two budgets can be used.

- One for planning and decision making, based on reasonable expectations **(expectations budget).**

- One for motivational purposes, with more difficult targets **(aspirations budget).**

Budgetary slack

> The difference between the minimum necessary costs and the costs built into the budget or actually incurred

Managers might deliberately overestimate costs and underestimate sales so that they will not be blamed for overspending and poor results.

A way of measuring performance which integrates traditional financial measures with operational, customer and staff issues. It is 'balanced' in the sense that managers are required to think in terms of all four perspectives, to prevent improvements being made in one area at the expense of another.

Perspective	Detail	Examples
Customer	Measures relating to what actually matters to customers (eg time, quality, performance of product)	■ Customer complaints ■ On-time deliveries
Internal business	Measures relating to the business processes that have the greatest impact on customer satisfaction (eg quality, employee skills)	■ Average set-up time ■ Quality control rejects
Innovation and learning	Measures to assess the organisation's capacity to maintain its competitive position through the acquisition of new skills/development of new products	■ Labour turnover rate ■ % of revenue generated by new products
Financial	Measures that consider the organisation from the shareholder's point of view	■ ROCE ■ EPS

Fixed budgets

These are prepared on the basis of an estimated volume of production and an estimated volume of sales. No variants of the budget are made to cover the event that actual and budgeted activity levels differ and they are not adjusted (in retrospect) to reflect actual activity levels.

Budgetary control

This is the practice of establishing budgets which identify areas of responsibility for individual managers and of regularly comparing actual results against expected results (using a flexible budget). The resulting variances provide guidelines for management control action.

Flexible budgets

These are budgets which, by recognising different cost behaviour patterns, change as activity levels change.

- At the planning stage, flexible budgets can be drawn up to show the effect of the actual volumes of output and sales differing from budgeted volumes.

- At the end of a period, actual results can be compared to a flexed budget *(what results should have been at actual output and sales volumes)* as a control procedure.

Example

Suppose that J Ltd has prepared budgeted profit forecasts based on 90%, 100% (50,000 units) and 105% activity.

| | Budgets | | | |
	90%	100%	105%	Actual (37,500 units sold)
	£	£	£	£
Revenue	1,350,000	1,500,000	1,575,000	1,075,000
Costs				
Materials	337,500	375,000	393,750	311,750
Labour	405,000	450,000	472,500	351,500
Production overhead	120,000	130,000	135,000	117,500
Admin overhead	70,000	70,000	70,000	66,500
	932,500	1,025,000	1,071,250	847,250
Profit	417,500	475,000	503,750	227,750

1. Decide whether costs are fixed, variable or semi-variable.

2. Split semi-variable costs into their fixed and variable components using the high-low method.

3. Flex the budget to the required activity level.

With **ABB**, **cost drivers** rather than volume of activity will be the bases for flexing the budget (see Chapter 10).

A budgetary control report for J Ltd is shown below.

	Flexed budget £	Actual £	Variance £
Revenue	1,125,000 (W1)	1,075,000	50,000 (A)
Costs			
Materials	281,250 (W2)	311,750	30,500 (A)
Labour	337,500 (W3)	351,500	14,000 (A)
Prod o/hd	105,000 (W4)	117,500	12,500 (A)
Admin o/hd	70,000 (W5)	66,500	3,500 (F)
	793,750	847,250	53,500 (A)
Profit	331,250	227,750	103,500 (A)

Workings

1   $37,500 \times (1,500,000/50,000)$

2   Material costs are variable.
    Costs per unit = £375,000/50,000 = £7.50
    Budget cost allowance = £7.50 × 37,500

3   Labour costs are variable.
    Cost per unit = £450,000/50,000 = £9
    Budget cost allowance = £9 × 37,500

4   Production overhead is a semi-variable cost
    At 90%, activity level = 50,000 × 0.9 = 45,000 units.
    Variable cost of (50,000 – 45,000) units = £(130,000 – 120,000).
    ∴ Variable cost per unit = £10,000/5,000 = £2.
    ∴ Fixed cost = £(130,000 – (50,000 × £2)) = £30,000
    Budget cost allowance = £(30,000 + (37,500 × £2))

5   Administration overhead is a fixed cost.

How can computers help with budgetary control?

- Calculation of flexed budget
- Detailed variance analysis
- Speedy production of control information

Budgetary control reports

Budget holders must receive these regularly so they can monitor the budget centre's operations and take necessary control action.

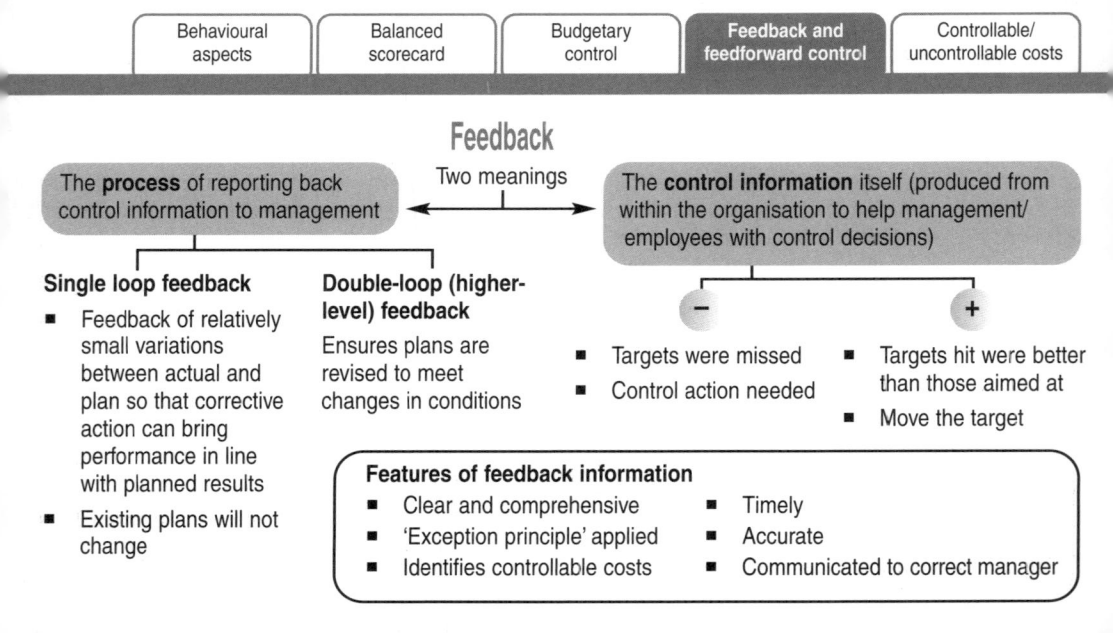

Feedback

Two meanings

The process of reporting back control information to management

The control information itself (produced from within the organisation to help management/ employees with control decisions)

Single loop feedback

- Feedback of relatively small variations between actual and plan so that corrective action can bring performance in line with planned results
- Existing plans will not change

Double-loop (higher-level) feedback

Ensures plans are revised to meet changes in conditions

−

- Targets were missed
- Control action needed

+

- Targets hit were better than those aimed at
- Move the target

Features of feedback information

- Clear and comprehensive
- 'Exception principle' applied
- Identifies controllable costs
- Timely
- Accurate
- Communicated to correct manager

Feedforward control

Control based on comparing original targets or actual results with a forecast of future results

1 Compare the **current forecast with the plan** to ascertain whether control action must be taken to get back to the plan.

2 Prepare a **revised forecast** to account for the effects of control action.

3 Compare the **revised forecast with the plan** to determine whether the plan will be achieved.

4 Compare the **original forecast with the revised forecast** to show the expected effect of control action.

5 At the end of the control period
- Compare **actual results with the revised forecast** (why did differences occur?)
- Compare **actual results with the plan** (how close are actual results to the plan?)

6 Prepare a **new forecast** and begin the control cycle again.

Managers of responsibility centres should only be held accountable for costs over which they have some influence. A distinction is therefore made between controllable and uncontrollable costs.

- **Most variable costs** are controllable in the short term.

- Some **fixed costs** are discretionary but most are uncontrollable in the short term.

- **Directly attributable fixed costs** are fixed in the short term within the relevant range but a drastic reduction in a department's output, say, would reduce/remove them.

- A cost **uncontrollable by a junior manager** might be **controllable by a senior manager** (eg overtime).

- A cost **uncontrollable by a manger in one department** may be **controllable by a manager in another** (see example).

Example

An increase in material costs might be caused by buying at higher prices than expected (controllable by the purchasing department) or by excessive wastage/spoilage (controllable by the production department).

Topic List

Changing business environment

AMT

Production management strategies

JIT systems

Synchronous manufacturing and WCM

TQM

Role of standard costing

In recent years, the impact of global competition, shorter product life cycles and the need to satisfy customers has led to new management approaches, more sophisticated manufacturing systems and investment in technology.

Key questions to try in the kit: 51,55
Refer to MCQ cards: 92-95

Changing competitive environment

	Then	**Now**
Manufacturing organisations	Pre 1970s, there was little overseas competition, costs were passed on to customers, minimal efforts were made to maximise efficiency/reduce costs/improve management practices.	There is massive overseas competition, and global networks for acquiring raw materials and distributing high quality, low-priced goods.
Service organisations	Pre 1980s, many were government-owned monopolies or protected by highly regulated, non-competitive environments. Cost increases were covered by increasing prices. Cost systems were not deemed necessary.	Privatisation and deregulation has resulted in intense competition, an increasing product range and a need for sophisticated costing systems.
Product life cycles	Organisations could rely on years of high demand for products.	Competitive environment, technological innovation and discriminating and sophisticated customer demand require continual product redesign and quick time to market.

Changing customer requirements

Successful organisations make customer satisfaction their priority.

Key success factors

- Cost efficiency
- Quality
- Time
- Innovation

New management approaches

- Continuous improvement
- Employee empowerment
- Total value chain analysis

Changing manufacturing systems

Traditional manufacturing systems

- Jobbing industries
- Batch processing
- Mass/flow production

Recent developments

- Group technology/repetitive manufacturing
- Dedicated cell layout

> Manufacturing processes must be sufficiently flexible both to accommodate new product design and to satisfy the demand for greater product diversity.

Computer-aided design (CAD)

- The effects of changing product specifications can be explored.
- Designs can be assessed in terms of cost and simplicity.
- Databases can match required and existing parts to reduce parts required and minimise stockholdings.

Flexible manufacturing systems (FMS)

- An FMS is a highly automated manufacturing system characterised by small batch production, the ability to change quickly from one job to another and very fast response times.
- Features include JIT, CIM, MHS and ASRs.

Computer-aided manufacturing (CAM)

- CAM includes robots, CNC machines, AGVs and ASRs.
- The ultimate aim is a set-up time of zero.
- It allows production in very small batch sizes (so that the production schedule is driven by customer requirements).

Electronic data interchange (EDI)

EDI facilitates communications between an organisation and its customers/suppliers by electronic transfer of information.

The **traditional approach** to determining materials requirements is to monitor the level of stocks constantly so that once they fall to a preset level they can be re-ordered. This ignores relationships between different stock lines (demand for a particular item is dependent on demand for assemblies/subassemblies of which it forms a part).

Modern computer techniques integrate such relationships into the stock ordering process.

- **Materials requirement planning (MRPI)**
  Focuses on materials

- **Manufacturing resource planning (MRPII)**
  Considers labour and machine requirements too

- **Enterprise resource planning (ERP)**
  Accounting-orientated information systems that identify and plan the enterprise-wide resources needed to take, make, distribute and account for customer orders

- ERP may also incorporate transactions with an organisation's suppliers and they help large national and multinational companies in particular to manage geographically-dispersed and complex operations.

- **Optimised production technology (OPT)**
  Seeks to optimise the use of bottleneck resources

Traditional responses to the problems of improving manufacturing capacity and reducing unit costs of production

- Longer production runs
- Economic batch quantities
- Fewer products in the product range
- More overtime
- Reduced time on preventative maintenance, to keep production flowing

Just-in-time systems challenge such 'traditional' views.

Although often described as a technique, JIT is more of a philosophy since it encompasses a commitment to continuous improvement and a search for excellence in the design and operation of the production management system.

Aims of JIT

- Minimise warehousing and storage costs.

- Eliminate waste by maintaining control over quality of stocks input to the production process.

- Reduce the amount of raw materials and WIP carried as working capital through more effective production planning.

- Reduce the amount of finished goods held as working capital.

Essential elements of JIT

- JIT purchasing
- Close relationships with suppliers
- Uniform loading
- Set-up time reduction
- Machine cells

- Quality
- Pull system (Kanban)
- Preventative maintenance
- Employee involvement
- Elimination of non-value-added costs

Problems with JIT

- Can be difficult to predict patterns of demand
- Makes the organisation vulnerable to disruptions in the supply chain
- Wide geographical spread makes its operation difficult

Value-added costs

Incurred for an activity that cannot be eliminated without the customer perceiving a deterioration in the performance, function or other quality of a product

Value is only added while a product is actually being processed.

8: The modern business environment

Synchronous manufacturing

This is a manufacturing philosophy which aims to ensure that all operations are performed for the common good of the organisation. It therefore requires managers to focus on areas which offer the greatest possibilities for global improvements rather than to attempt to improve the process everywhere in the system (the JIT philosophy).

> When answering questions on the modern business environment, keep in mind the whole time that organisations have to be *flexible* enough to provide *reliable* products *quickly*.

World Class Manufacturing (WCM)

> 'The manufacture of high-quality products reaching customers quickly (or the delivery of a prompt and quality service) at a low cost to provide high performance and customer satisfaction.'
> *(Clarke)*

Key elements of WCM

- Achieving 100% quality
- JIT manufacturing
- Managing people (multiskilling, teamwork, empowerment)
- Response to customers (knowing their requirements, supplying on time, responding to changes in needs)

Total Quality Management (TQM)

> The process of focusing on quality in the management of *all* resources and relationships within the organisation

Two basic principles of TQM

Getting things right first time, on the basis that the cost of correcting mistakes is greater than the cost of preventing them from happening in the first place

Continuous improvement – the belief that it is always possible to improve, no matter how high quality may be already

Measuring and controlling quality

1. **Quality assurance** (supplier guarantees quality)
2. **Inspection of output** (at various key stages)
3. **Monitoring customer reaction** (involves monitoring complaints in the form of letters, returned goods, requests for servicing and so on)

Employees and quality

- Workers are **empowered** and encouraged to become **multiskilled.**
- Workers are encouraged to **take responsibility** for their work.

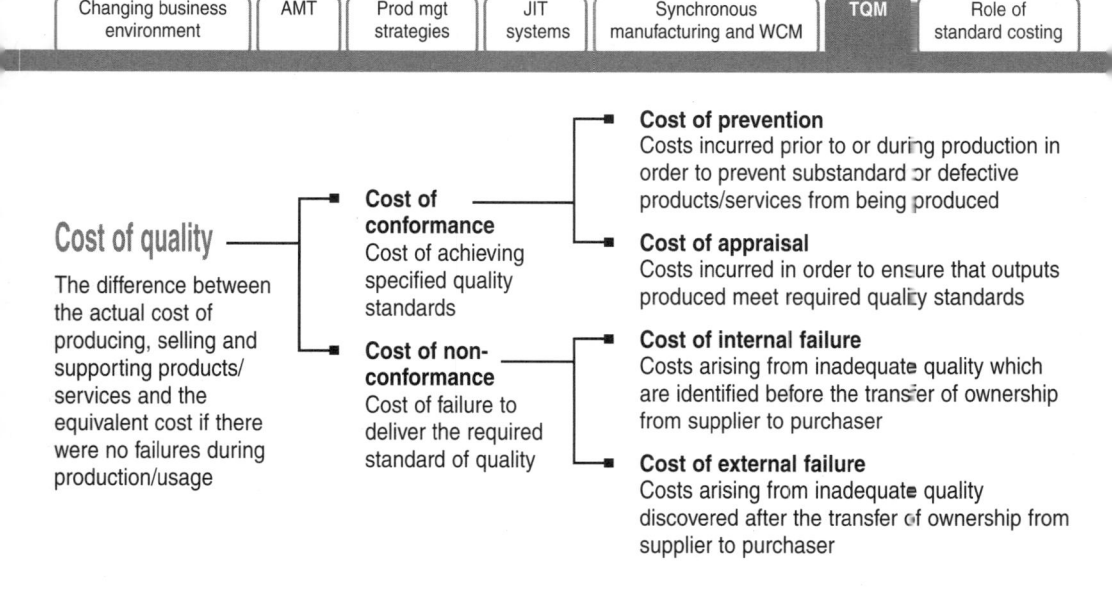

Cost of quality

The difference between the actual cost of producing, selling and supporting products/services and the equivalent cost if there were no failures during production/usage

Cost of conformance
Cost of achieving specified quality standards

Cost of non-conformance
Cost of failure to deliver the required standard of quality

Cost of prevention
Costs incurred prior to or during production in order to prevent substandard or defective products/services from being produced

Cost of appraisal
Costs incurred in order to ensure that outputs produced meet required quality standards

Cost of internal failure
Costs arising from inadequate quality which are identified before the transfer of ownership from supplier to purchaser

Cost of external failure
Costs arising from inadequate quality discovered after the transfer of ownership from supplier to purchaser

The cost of conformance is a discretionary cost incurred with the intention of eliminating non-conformance costs. The cost of non-conformance can only be reduced by increasing the cost of conformance. The optimal investment in conformance costs is when total costs of quality reach a minimum (which may be below 100% quality conformance).

Examples

Cost of prevention	Cost of appraisal	Cost of internal failure	Cost of external failure
Training in quality control	Inspection of goods inwards	Losses due to lower selling prices for sub-quality goods	Cost of customer service section

Cost of quality reports

- Such reports show how much is being spent on each of the categories.
- They indicate how total cost can be reduced by more sensible division of costs between the categories.
- Non-financial measures (eg number of warranty claims) may be more appropriate for lower-level managers.

8: The modern business environment

Criticisms of standard costing in today's environment

Standard costing has been described as unhelpful and potentially misleading in today's environment.

Standard costing

- Concentrates on a narrow range of costs
- Too much emphasis on direct labour costs
- Focuses on short-term variable costs
- Relies on repetitive operations and homogeneous output
- Requires stable conditions, and assumes performance to standard is acceptable
- Control statements produced weekly/monthly

Current environment

- Quality and customer satisfaction are important.
- Direct labour is a small proportion of costs.
- Most costs are fixed in the short term.
- Organisations must respond to customers' changing requirements.
- It is more dynamic and focused on continuous improvement.
- Control information is required promptly.

Standard costing in a total quality environment

Standard costing environment

- Stable, standardised, repetitive environment
- Planned level of scrap
- Predetermined standards
- Concentrates on quantity
- Effectiveness = high volume of output at low cost
- Failure is measured in variances
- Labour efficiency measured in terms of individual tasks and level of output
- Labour and material variances

Total quality environment

- Continual improvement
- Zero defects
- Continual improvements alter inputs, prices etc
- Quality is the issue
- Effectiveness = high quality output from high quality input
- Failure is measured in terms of internal/external failure costs
- Efficiency of labour (responsible multi-task teams) measured in terms of reworking, returns, defects
- Minimal labour rate variances (guaranteed weekly wage) and few material price/usage variances (fixed price contracts, supplier guaranteeing quality)

Standard costing and new technology

Standard costing has traditionally been associated with labour-intensive operations. Can it be applied to capital-intensive production?

- Labour costs are a small proportion of total costs, so would labour variances have any control value?

- Fixed costs are a significant proportion of total costs but there are questions over the relevance of fixed overhead variance control information.

- Machines are more accurate than human operators so material usage variances should be non-existent.

Standard costing and JIT

	Examples
Traditionally	Avoid idle time, keep up production and so minimise adverse efficiency variances.
JIT with TQM	Such action would lead to unwanted stocks.
Traditionally	Shop around for cheapest suppliers to minimise adverse material price variances.
JIT	Focus is on supplier reliability and quality, and on establishing long-term contractual links.

9: Absorption and marginal costing

Topic List

Absorption costing

Marginal costing

Absorption costing vs marginal costing

You will have covered the basics of these costing methods in your earlier studies but the Paper 8 syllabus requires you to have a thorough knowledge of the material.

Key question to try in the kit: 57
Refer to MCQ cards (with Chs 10 & 11)
                                    96-116

1 Allocation Process by which whole cost items are charged *direct* to a cost unit or cost centre (without the need for apportionment).

2 Apportionment First stage involves 'sharing out' overheads in general overhead cost centres (eg rent and rates) between the other cost centres using a fair basis (such as floor area occupied by each cost centre for rent and rates).

Second stage involves sharing out the (directly allocated and apportioned) costs within service cost centres to production cost centres.

Methods of service department cost apportionment

- Direct apportionment to production departments only
- Repeated distribution method
- Simultaneous equation (algebraic) method
- Step-wise (elimination) method

> **Apportioning service department overheads is only useful if the resulting product costs reflect accurately the amounts expended by service departments. If the apportionment is arbitrary or ill-considered, the product costs will be misleading.**

3 Absorption

Overhead absorption rate (OAR) = estimated overhead ÷ budgeted activity level

Example

Budgeted overhead: £100,000
Budgeted labour cost: £200,000 for 20,000 hrs
Budgeted output: 2,000 units
OARs: 50% of labour cost
£5 per labour hr
£50 per unit
Actual overhead: £110,000
Actual labour hours: 18,000 hrs

	£
Actual overhead	110,000
O/hd absorbed (18,000 × £5)	90,000
Under-absorbed overhead	20,000

Possible absorption bases

Choose the fairest.
- Per unit
- Per direct labour hr/machine hr
- % of direct material/labour/prime cost

Under/over absorption occurs because overhead absorbed is based on estimated expenditure and activity levels.

Under/over absorption

- O/hd incurred > o/hd absorbed ⟹ under-absorbed o/hd = adverse adjustment to P&L a/c
- O/hd incurred < o/hd absorbed ⟹ over-absorbed o/hd = favourable adjustment to P&L a/c

Three major principles

1 Variable costs are charged to the cost of making / selling a product, fixed costs are charged direct to the profit and loss account.

2 Stock is valued at variable production cost (not full production cost as with absorption costing).

3 Profit = total contribution (difference between sales revenue and *all* variable costs) – period fixed costs.

If the opening and closing stock values differ, the difference in profits using the two methods equals the difference in the fixed overhead included in the absorption costing opening and closing stock valuations.

If the opening stock values are greater than closing stock values, marginal costing shows the greater profit.

In the long run, profit is the same whatever method is used.

Example

Opening stock: 100 units

Closing stock: 195 units

Fixed OAR = £17 per unit

Marginal costing profit = £73,500

Absorption costing profit is therefore higher and equals £73,500 + ((195 – 100) × £17) = £75,115

Profit statements

Absorption costing

	£	£
Sales		X
Opening stock (at full cost)	X	
Full prod'n costs (var + abs'd fixed o/hd)	X	
Less closing stock (at full cost)	X	
Production cost of sales	X	
Under/over-absorbed overhead	X	
Total costs		X
Gross profit		X
Other costs		X
Net profit		X

Marginal costing

	£	£
Sales		X
Opening stock (at variable cost)	X	
Variable production costs	X	
Less closing stock (at variable cost)	X	
Variable prod'n cost of sales		X
Contribution		X
Fixed production costs		X
Gross profit		X
Other costs		X
Net profit		X

Reconciling profit figures

The figures given by the two methods

	£
Marginal costing profit	X
Adjust for fixed overhead in stock	
+ Stock increase in units × fixed overhead absorbed per unit	X
OR	
– Stock decrease in units × fixed overhead absorbed per unit	
Absorption costing profit	X̲

The profits for different periods

■ **Marginal costing**

	£
Marginal costing profit for period 1	X
+ Increase in contribution from higher sales volume in period 2	
OR	X
– Fall in contribution from lower sales volume in period 2	
Marginal costing profit for period 2	X̲

■ **Absorption costing**

	£
Absorption costing profit for period 1	X
+ Increase in profit/–decrease in profit due to change in sales volume	X
Adjustments for under/over absorption:	
(1) – over absorption in period 1 or + under absorption in period 1	X
(2) + over absorption in period 2 or – under absorption in period 2	X
Absorption costing profit for period 2	X̲

Arguments in favour of absorption costing	Arguments in favour of marginal costing
■ When sales fluctuate because of seasonality in sales demand but production is held constant, absorption costing avoids large fluctuations in profit.	■ It shows how an organisation's cash flows and profits are affected by changes in sales volumes since contribution varies in direct proportion to units sold.
■ Marginal costing fails to recognise the importance of working to full capacity and its effects on pricing decisions if a cost plus method of pricing is being used.	■ By using absorption costing and setting a production level greater than sales demand, profits can be manipulated.
■ Prices based on marginal cost (minimum prices) do not guarantee that contribution will cover fixed costs.	■ Separating fixed and variable costs is vital for decision making.
■ In the long run all costs are variable, and absorption costing recognises these long-run variable costs.	■ For short-run decisions in which fixed costs do not change (such as short-run tactical decisions seeking to make the best use of existing resources), the decision rule is to choose the alternative which maximises *contribution*, fixed costs being irrelevant.
■ It is consistent with the requirements of SSAP 9.	

Topic List

Reasons for development

ABC systems

Merits and criticisms

ABB

Throughput accounting

Don't be daunted by these modern approaches. Remember that activity based costing is simply an alternative to traditional absorption costing, while throughput accounting is just a costing system particularly suited to a specific environment (one in which JIT is being used).

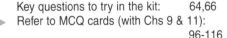

Key questions to try in the kit: 64,66
Refer to MCQ cards (with Chs 9 & 11):
96-116

Modern manufacturing environment

- An increase in support services (such as production scheduling)
  - These services assist in the manufacture of a wide range of products.
  - They are unaffected by changes in production volume.
  - They vary instead with the range and complexity of products.
- An increase in overheads as a proportion of total costs

Inadequacies of absorption costing

- Implies all overheads are related to production volume
- Developed at a time when organisations produced only a narrow range of products and when overheads were only a small fraction of total costs
- Tends to allocate too great a proportion of overheads to high-volume products (which cause relatively little diversity) and too small a proportion to low-volume products (which cause greater diversity and use more support services)

Outline of an ABC system

1 Identify an organisation's major activities.

2 Identify **cost drivers**. ━━━━━━━━━━┓

3 Collect the costs associated with each activity into **cost pools**.

4 Charge costs of each cost pool to products on the basis of products' usage of the activity (measured by number of the activity's cost driver a product generates) using a cost driver rate (total costs in cost pool ÷ number of cost drivers).

Cost drivers

┗━ Any factor which causes a change in the cost of an activity

Examples

The cost driver for a cost that varies with production volume in the short term (such as power costs) should be volume related (eg labour hours or machine hours).

The cost driver for a cost that is related to the transactions undertaken by the support department where the cost is incurred should be the transaction in the support department (such as the number of production runs for the cost of setting up production runs).

10: Activity based costing and throughput accounting

Example

Cost of goods inwards department totalled £10,000. Cost driver for goods inwards activity is number of deliveries. During 20X0 there were 1,000 deliveries. 200 of these deliveries related to product X. 2,000 units of product X were produced

Cost per unit of cost driver

$$= £10,000/1,000$$
$$= £10$$

Cost of activity attributable to product X

$$= £10 \times 200$$
$$= £2,000$$

Cost of activity per unit of product X

$$= £2,000/2,000$$
$$= £1$$

When should ABC be introduced?

If the additional information it provides results in action that increases organisational profitability, which occurs if......

ABC analysis differs significantly from absorption costing analysis, which occurs if......

- production overheads are high in relation to direct costs (especially labour), or
- overhead resource consumption is not just driven by production volume, or
- there is wide variety in the product range, or
- overhead resource input varies significantly across the product range

Transactions analysis

- **Logistical transactions** Activities concerned with organising the flow of resources throughout the manufacturing process
- **Balancing transactions** Activities which ensure that demand for and supply of resources are matched
- **Quality transactions** Activities which relate to ensuring that production is at the required level of quality
- **Change transactions** Activities associated with ensuring that customers' requirements are met

The primary driver of these activities (which cause overheads to be incurred) is not normally production volume.

Analysis of activities

Costs of...	such as...	are dependent on...
Unit level activities	machine power	volume of production
Batch level activities	set-up costs	number of batches
Product level activities	product management	existence of a product group/line
Facility level activities	rent and rates	organisation simply being in business

If most overheads are related to unit level/facility level activities, costs determined using ABC and absorption costing will be similar. If overheads are associated with batch/product level activities, however, they will be significantly different.

Merits

- ☑ Simple (once information is obtained)
- ☑ Recognises the complexity of modern manufacturing with its multiple cost drivers
- ☑ Facilitates a good understanding of what drives overhead costs
- ☑ Concerned not just with production costs but *all* overhead costs
- ☑ Helps with cost control (because by controlling the incidence of the cost driver, the level of cost can be controlled)
- ☑ Can help with cost management
- ☑ Can be used in conjunction with customer profitability analysis

Criticisms

- ☒ ABC is more complex than absorption costing and so should only be introduced if it provides additional management information
- ☒ Cost drivers might be difficult to identify
- ☒ Can one cost driver explain the behaviour of all items in a cost pool?
- ☒ Some measure of arbitrary cost apportionment is still needed for costs such as rent and rates

Activity based budgeting (ABB)

At its **simplest**, ABB is the use of costs determined using ABC as a basis for preparing budgets.

More **formally**

- The definition of the activities that underlie the financial figures in each function
- The use of the level of activity to decide how much resource should be allocated, how well it is being managed and to explain variances from budget

Flexed budgets using ABC data

Build budget cost allowances for activities on the basis of a budgeted cost per unit of cost driver and a budgeted number of cost drivers

- All costs are therefore variable (in that they vary in line with the incidence of the cost driver) and so are more readily controlled.
- Implications of increases/decreases in levels of activity are immediately apparent.

10: Activity based costing and throughput accounting

Theory of constraints (TOC)

An **approach to production management** which aims to maximise sales revenue less material and variable overhead costs. It focuses on the factors which act as constraints to this maximisation.

Binding constraint

A process that acts as a bottleneck (or limiting factor) and constrains throughput

Principles

Stock costs money in terms of storage space and interest and so is undesirable.

- The only stock that should be held is a buffer stock immediately prior to the bottleneck so that output through it is never held up.

- Operations prior to the binding constraint should operate at the same speed as the binding constraint otherwise WIP will build up.

Aim

Maximise **throughput contribution** (sales revenue less material cost) while keeping **conversion cost** (all operating costs accept material cost) and **investment cost** (stock, equipment, building costs etc) to a minimum.

TOC is not an accounting system. It is a production system.

Throughput accounting (TA)

An **approach to accounting**, in line with the JIT philosophy, which assumes management have a given set of resources available (existing buildings, capital equipment, labour force). Using these resources, purchased materials and parts must be processed to generate sales revenue. The most appropriate financial objective to set is therefore maximisation of throughput (sales revenue less direct material cost).

Why is TA different?

TA differs from other accounting systems because of what it **emphasises**.

1st **Throughput**

2nd **Stock minimisation**

3rd **Cost control**

Examples

Throughput accounting can be used successfully in service and retail industries.

- If there is a delay in processing a potential customer's application, business can be lost.

- A bottleneck might form if work that could be done by nurses has to be carried out by doctors.

Three concepts upon which TA is based

1 All factory costs except materials costs are fixed.

2 The ideal inventory level is zero (apart from a buffer stock prior to the bottleneck) and so unavoidable idle capacity is inevitable.

3 No value is added and no profit is made until a sale takes place.

Factors that limit throughput

- Bottleneck resources
- Lack of product quality/reliability
- Unreliable material supplies
- Customers with particular demands

Throughput measures

- **Return per time period**
  Production priority is given to the products best able to generate throughput and hence it is given to those products that maximise throughput contribution or return per time period (where **throughput contribution** or **return = sales revenue – material costs**).Rank on the basis of **return ÷ time (in hrs or mins) on bottleneck resource**.

- **TA ratio**
  Unlike return per time period, this takes into consideration the costs involved in running the factory. Rank on the basis of **return per time period ÷ conversion cost per time period**

- **Effectiveness ratio**
  Standard minutes of throughput achieved ÷ minutes available

Example

Product X requires ten machine hours. Machine time is the bottleneck resource as only 1,500 hours are available each week.

Product X sells for £320 per unit and has a direct material cost of £120 per unit. Total factory costs are £25,000 per week.

Return per factory hour = return ÷ time on bottleneck resource = £(320 − 120) ÷ 10 = £20

TA ratio = return per factory hour ÷ cost per factory hour

= £20 ÷ (£25,000 ÷ 1,500) = 1.2

10: Activity based costing and throughput accounting

Criticisms

- It is seen by some as too short term, as all costs other than direct material cost are regarded as fixed.
- It concentrates on direct material cost and does not control other costs.
- By attempting to maximise throughput an organisation could be producing in excess of profit-maximising output.

Advantages

The principal advantage of TA is that it directs attention to critical factors.

- Bottlenecks
- Key elements in making profit
- Inventory reduction
- Reducing response time to customer demand
- Even production flow
- Overall effectiveness and efficiency

Topic List

Losses in process

Valuing opening and closing WIP

Joint products and by-products

Again, you have already covered these topics at an introductory level, but for Paper 8 you will need to be aware of higher-level issues and be able to perform more complex calculations.

Key questions to try in the kit: 56,60
Refer to MCQ cards (with Chs 9 & 10):
96-116

Four-step approach to answering questions

1 Determine output and losses

2 Calculate cost per unit of output, losses and WIP

3 Calculate total cost of output, losses and WIP

4 Complete accounts

Accounting for losses

No costs are charged to units of normal loss (which, if relevant, are valued at their scrap value).

Units of abnormal loss/gain are valued at full cost per unit =

$$\frac{\text{Total process costs} - \text{scrap proceeds of normal loss}}{\text{Expected units of output}}$$

Losses with a disposal cost

- Increase the process costs by the cost of disposing of units of normal loss.
- Use the resulting cost per unit to value good output and abnormal loss/gain.
- Include the disposal costs of the normal loss units on the debit side of the process a/c and the disposal costs of the abnormal loss units on the debit side of the abnormal loss a/c.

Scrap value of loss

Deduct the scrap value of normal loss from the cost of materials when performing step 2 of the four-step approach.

PROCESS A/C	£		£	* A process a/c would not
Costs	X	Finished output	X	normally include
		Normal loss *(valued at scrap value)*	X	abnormal loss and
Abnormal gain* (valued at full cost per unit)	X	Abnormal loss* (valued at full cost per unit)	X	abnormal gain
	X		X	

ABNORMAL LOSS A/C	£		£
Process a/c	X	Scrap a/c	X
		P & L a/c	X
	X		X

SCRAP A/C	£		£
Scrap value of:		Cash proceeds	X
normal loss	X	Scrap value of	
abnormal loss	X	abnormal gain	X
	X		X

Weighted average method

No distinction is made between units of opening WIP and new units introduced. The cost of opening WIP is added to costs incurred during the period and completed units of opening WIP are each given a value of one full equivalent unit of production.

1

Statement of equivalent units

	Units		Equiv units
Opening WIP completed	500	(100%)	500
Fully worked units	2,200	(100%)	2,200
Finished output	2,700		2,700
Closing WIP	300	(80%)	240
	3,000		2,940

2

Statement of cost per equivalent unit

$$\frac{\text{Costs b/f in opening WIP} + \text{costs incurred in period}}{\text{Equivalent units}} = \frac{£(2,800 + 26,400)}{2,940} = £9.932$$

3

Statement of evaluation

	Equiv units	Valuation £
Output to finished goods	2,700 × £9.932	26,816
Closing WIP	240 × £9.932	2,384
		29,200

4

Process a/c

	Units	£		Units	£
Op. WIP	500	2,800	Fin. goods	2,700	26,816
Materials	2,500	20,000	Cl WIP	300	2,384
Conv. cost	-	6,400		-	-
	3,000	29,200		3,000	29,200

FIFO method

1 | **Statement of equivalent units**

	Units		Equiv units
Opening WIP completed	500	*(40%)	200
Fully worked units	2,200	(100%)	2,200
Finished output	2,700		2,400
Closing WIP	300	(80%)	240
	3,000		2,640

* % of work required to *complete* op. WIP

2 | **Statement of cost per equivalent unit**

$$\frac{\text{Costs incurred in period}}{\text{Equivalent units}} = \frac{£26,400 \text{ (say)}}{2,640} = £10$$

3 | **Statement of evaluation**

	Equiv units	Valuation £
Opening WIP completed	200	2,000
Fully worked units	2,200	22,000
Closing WIP	240	2,400
		26,400

4 | **Process a/c**

	Units	£		Units	£
Op. WIP	500	*2,800	Finished goods:		
Materials	2,500	6,400	Op. WIP	500	**4,800
			Fully worked		
Conv. cost		20,000	units	2,200	22,000
	3,000	29,200		2,700	26,800
			Cl. WIP	300	2,400
				3,000	29,200

* B/f value of op. WIP from previous period (say)

** £2,800 (b/f) + £2,000 (current period)

FIFO stock valuation is more common than the weighted average method, so you should use it in the exam unless given an indication to the contrary. But apply the following rules if you are given limited information about opening stock.

- *FIFO method* if given the degree of completion of each element of opening stock
- *Weighted average method* if given the value of each element of opening stock

Equivalent units and losses

If loss occurs at the end of processing

- A unit of normal loss counts as no equivalent units

- A unit of abnormal loss = +1 equivalent unit

- A unit of abnormal gain = –1 equivalent unit

- If loss has a scrap value and completion percentages are different for each input, deduct the scrap value of normal loss from the cost of materials (or, where appropriate, from the cost of materials input from the previous process).

If loss occurs before the end of processing

Units of loss/gain count as a proportion of an equivalent unit, according to work done/ material added at point of inspection. If loss occurs gradually, both opening and closing WIP will have suffered some but not all of the loss already and so the calculation of equivalent units must take this into account to be fair.

Joint products

Two or more products output from the same processing operation but indistinguishable up to the point of separation and having a substantial sales revenue (possibly after further processing)

Apportioning joint/common costs

Costs incurred up to the point of separation (**split-off point**) need to be apportioned between the joint products for the purposes of stock valuation, profitability analysis and pricing.

Joint product costs are not used for decision making.

There are four methods of apportioning joint/common costs.

By-products

Produced at the same time and from the same process as main/joint products but having a relatively low sales value in comparison

- They are recognised by their relatively low sales value.
- If the by-product is a normal occurrence, reduce process costs by the net realisable value of the by-product.
- If a one-off, treat the net realisable value of the by-product as miscellaneous income in the P&L account.

11: Process costing

Method 1: Physical measurement

- Cost is apportioned on the basis of the proportion that the output of each product bears by weight or volume to the total output.
- It is unsuitable where products separate during processing into different states.
- It ignores sales value and may lead to inappropriate results if sales values and volumes differ significantly.

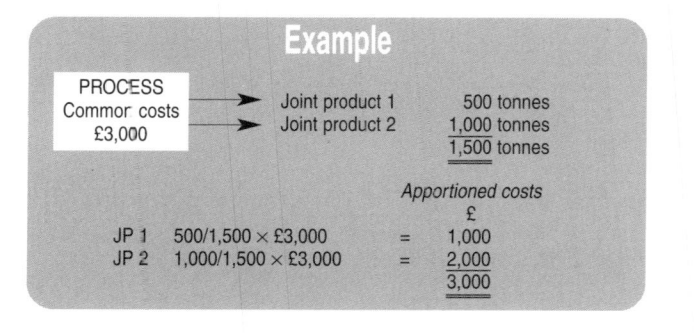

	Example	
PROCESS Common costs £3,000	Joint product 1	500 tonnes
	Joint product 2	1,000 tonnes
		1,500 tonnes

Apportioned costs
£

JP 1	500/1,500 × £3,000	=	1,000
JP 2	1,000/1,500 × £3,000	=	2,000
			3,000

Method 2: Sales value at split-off point

Cost is apportioned according to products' abilities to produce income (that is, in the proportions that the sales values of the products bear to the sales value of the process's total output).

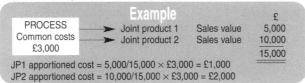

Example

			£
PROCESS Common costs £3,000	→ Joint product 1	Sales value	5,000
	→ Joint product 2	Sales value	10,000
			15,000

JP1 apportioned cost = 5,000/15,000 × £3,000 = £1,000
JP2 apportioned cost = 10,000/15,000 × £3,000 = £2,000

Method 3: Sales value minus further processing costs

If the sales value at split-off point is not available, costs can be apportioned on the basis of residual / notional / proxy sales value (final sales value minus further processing costs).

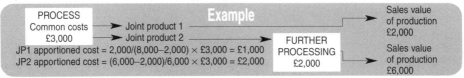

Example

PROCESS Common costs £3,000 → Joint product 1 ——————————————→ Sales value of production £2,000

→ Joint product 2 ——————→ FURTHER PROCESSING £2,000 → Sales value of production £6,000

JP1 apportioned cost = 2,000/(8,000–2,000) × £3,000 = £1,000
JP2 apportioned cost = (6,000–2,000)/6,000 × £3,000 = £2,000

Method 4: Weighted average method

If 'units' of joint product are not comparable in terms of physical resemblance or physical weight (gas, liquid, solid etc), common costs are apportioned on the basis of 'weighted units' (units of joint product × weighting factor).

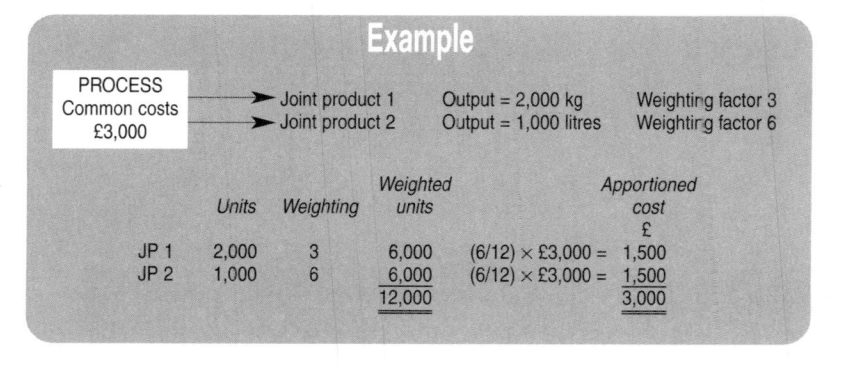

Example

| PROCESS Common costs £3,000 | Joint product 1 | Output = 2,000 kg | Weighting factor 3 |
| | Joint product 2 | Output = 1,000 litres | Weighting factor 6 |

	Units	Weighting	Weighted units		Apportioned cost £
JP 1	2,000	3	6,000	(6/12) × £3,000 =	1,500
JP 2	1,000	6	6,000	(6/12) × £3,000 =	1,500
			12,000		3,000

12: Cost reduction

Topic List

This chapter covers general methods of reducing costs as well as the specific techniques of value analysis and functional analysis.

Key questions to try in the kit: 46,53
Refer to MCQ cards: 117-118

Cost reduction

A planned and positive approach to reducing expenditure

Note the contrast with cost **control**, which is concerned with keeping the costs of operating a business within acceptable limits.

Approaches

1. Crash programmes to cut spending levels
   - Often introduced in times of crisis
   - Can imply panic and/or authoritarian approach
   - Can be too little, too late or misdirected

2. Planned (continuous, long-term) programmes to reduce costs

Scope of cost reduction campaigns

- Should embrace the activities of the entire organisation
- Should have a long-term aim and short-term objectives

Difficulties

- Resistance from employees
- Often introduced as rushed, desperate measures
- Costs are reduced in one cost centre, but extra costs appear in another

Improving efficiency

- Improve **materials usage** by reducing waste
  - □ Use better quality materials
  - □ Introduce new equipment
- Improve **labour productivity**
  - □ Pay incentives
  - □ Change work methods
  - □ Improve cooperation between groups/departments
  - □ Introduce new standards
- Improve efficiency of **equipment usage**
  - □ Increase preventative maintenance
  - □ Make better use of resources

> **Once costs have been reduced by improving efficiency, cost control must be applied by management.**

Other ways to reduce costs

Reducing materials costs

- Obtaining lower prices for purchases
- Improving stores control and reducing stores costs
- Using alternative materials
- Standardising parts

Reducing finance costs

- Take advantage of discounts for early payment
- Reconsider policies for offering early payment discounts
- Reassess sources of finance
- Improve foreign exchange dealings

Other methods include **rationalisation measures** and **control over spending decisions**.

Reducing labour costs

- Replace humans with machinery.

- **Work study**, which has two main parts, is a means of raising productivity by reorganisation of work.

- **Organisation and methods (O&M)** is a generic term for those techniques, including method study and work measurement, that are used in examining clerical, administrative and management procedures and organisation to effect improvement.

- Improve efficiency/productivity (see page 115).

Example

Dealing with customer complaints is a non-value-added activity which can only be eliminated if the causes of the complaints are eliminated.

- **Method study** is the recording and critical examination of existing and proposed ways of doing work as a means of developing and applying easier and more effective methods and reducing costs.

- **Work measurement** is the process of establishing the time for a qualified worker to carry out a specified job at a specified level of performance.

Value-added/non-value-added activities

Value is added when an activity results in a change to a product/service that the ultimate customer deems valuable and hence is willing to pay for.

Non-value-added activities are frequently caused by inadequacies in existing processes and can only be eliminated if the inadequacies are addressed.

Value analysis (VA) is a planned, scientific approach to cost reduction which reviews the material composition of a product and the production design so that modifications and improvements can be made which do not reduce the value of the product to the customer/user.

Benefits
- Lower costs
- Better products
- Higher profits

are achieved by
- cost elimination/prevention
- cost reduction
- improving product quality and so selling more at the same price
- improving product quality and so increasing selling price

Aspects of a product's value to consider

- **Cost** value – cost of producing/selling it
- **Exchange** value – its market value
- **Use** value – what it does
- **Esteem** value – prestige customer attaches to it

Conventional cost reduction techniques v **Value analysis**

Try to achieve the lowest production cost for a specific product design

Tries to find the least cost method of making a product that achieves its desired function

Typical considerations in VA

- Can a cheaper (but as good or better) substitute material be found?
- Can unnecessary weight or embellishments be removed without reducing the product's attractiveness or desirability?
- Is it possible to use standardised or fewer components?

Functional analysis

This is most commonly applied during the development stage of products and uses the functions of a product/service (such as 'to make a mark' for a pen) as the basis for cost management.

Value engineering

The application of similar techniques to those of VA to new products, with the aim of designing and developing new products of a given value at minimum cost

Steps in a VA study

1. Select a product/service for investigation.
2. Obtain and record information about it.
3. Analyse this information and evaluate the product, considering each aspect of value in turn.
4. Consider alternatives.
5. Select the least-cost alternative for recommending to management.
6. Make a recommendation.
7. If accepted, implement the recommendation.
8. After a period, evaluate the outcome and measure the cost savings.

13: Relevant costs and decision making

Topic List

Relevant costing

Types of decision

Don't focus solely on the numerical aspects of decision-making questions. Written parts (covering qualitative aspects of decisions, further considerations to take into account and so on) are just as important.

Key question to try in the kit: 73
Refer to MCQ cards: 119-122

Relevant costs

Relevant costs are future, incremental cash flows.

They include **avoidable** and **opportunity** costs and **directly attributable fixed costs**.

Non-relevant costs

- **Sunk** costs
- **Committed** costs
- **Notional** costs
- **Historical** costs
- **General fixed** costs

Assumptions in relevant costing

- Cost behaviour patterns are known.
- Costs, prices and demand are known with certainty.
- The objective in the short run is to maximise 'satisfaction' (short-term profit).
- Information is complete and reliable.

Qualitative factors in decision making

- Availability of cash
- Inflation
- Employees
- Customers
- Competitors
- Timing factors
- Suppliers
- Feasibility
- Unquantified opportunity costs
- Flexibility and internal control

Relevant cost of materials

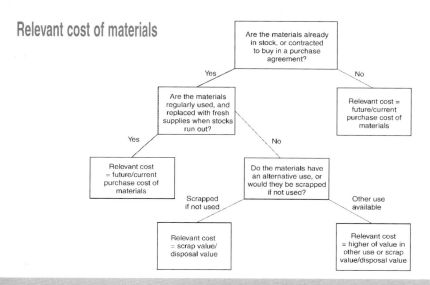

Accepting or rejecting special orders

An order should only be accepted if it increases contribution and hence profit.

Joint product decisions

If joint products can be sold either at split-off point *or* after further processing, the decision should be based on whether the increase in revenue is greater than post-separation processing costs.

Joint/common costs are irrelevant to the decision.

Make or buy decisions

A make or buy problem involves a decision by an organisation about whether it should either make a product using its own resources or pay another organisation to make the product.

When there are no limiting factors, relevant costs are the differential costs between the two options (which frequently consist of differences in unit variable costs plus differences in directly attributable fixed costs).

Other considerations

- 'Make' option gives management direct control of work
- 'Buy' option has the benefit of subcontractors' skill and expertise but need to assess their reliability
- Possible uses of spare capacity if a subcontractor is used (and there are no scarce resources)

Shutdown decisions

Qualitative factors relating to the impact on employees, customers, competitors and suppliers must be considered.

Extra shift decisions

The decision to work an extra shift and incur additional costs (overtime, shift premium, heating) should be taken on the basis of whether the additional benefits are greater than the additional costs.

Qualitative factors

- Will the workforce be willing to work overtime and if so, what will it cost?

- Do extra hours have to be worked just to remain competitive?

- Will extra hours increase revenue or will there simply be a change in the demand pattern?

13: Relevant costs and decision making

Notes

Topic List

Decisions involving one limiting factor

Decisions involving restricted freedom of action

Make or buy decisions and scarce resources

Limiting factors and opportunity costs

Assumptions and further considerations

A resource (such as labour or materials) which limits production to a level below demand is known as a limiting (or key) factor. It is assumed in limiting factor analysis (a technique for determining the optimum product mix) that management will select a profit-maximising product mix and that profit is maximised when contribution is maximised (given no change in fixed cost expenditure).

Key questions to try in the kit: 71,75,78
Refer to MCQ cards: 123-127

Scenario	How to maximise contribution/profit	Detail
Sales demand restricts greater production/output	Make exactly the amount required for sales (and no more) provided that each product sold earns a positive contribution.	
One scarce resource (such as material or labour)	Earn the biggest possible contribution per unit of scarce resource (see example below).	Assume fixed costs remain unchanged whatever the production mix, the only relevant costs being variable costs.
One limiting factor and restrictions on sales demand	Rank products in order of contribution-earning ability per unit of limiting factor but produce the top-ranked products up to the sales demand limit.	Although there may appear to be more than one scarce resource, it may be that there is no limiting factor except sales demand or that there is only one scarce resource that prevents full potential sales demand being achieved.

An examination problem might present you with a situation in which there is a limiting factor, without specifically stating so, and you will have the task of recognising what the situation is. You may be given a hint with the wording of the question.

For example, a question in the May 2001 exam stated that 'it has been estimated that the consultants will be able to work for a total of 2,400 days during the year'.

If you suspect the existence of a limiting factor, some quick computations should confirm your suspicions.

1. Calculate the amount of the scarce resource (material quantities, labour hours, machine hours and so on) needed to meet the potential sales demand.

2. Calculate the amount of the scarce resource available (for example number of employees multiplied by maximum working hours per employee).

3. Compare the two figures. Obviously, if the resources needed exceed the resources available, there is a limiting factor on output and sales.

Example

L Ltd sells two products, the T and the J.

	T £	J £
Direct labour (£5 per hour)	15	10
Direct materials (£2 per kg)	2	5
Variable overheads	2	2
Fixed overheads	3	3
	22	20
Selling price	£25	£24
Maximum demand	10,000	8,000
Maximum availability of labour		40,000 hrs

1 Confirm limiting factor is *not* sales.

Labour hours required to fulfil demand = $(10,000 \times 3) + (8,000 \times 2) = 46,000$, which means there is a shortfall of 6,000 hours.

2 Calculate the contribution per unit of scarce resource.

	T	J
Unit contribution	£(25 – 19) £6	£(24 – 17) £7
Labour hours per unit	3	2
Contribution per labour hour	£2	£3.50
Rank	2nd	1st

3 Work out budgeted production and sales.

Product	Hours	Production	Cont'n per unit £	Total cont'n £
J	(8,000 × 2) = 16,000	(÷ 2) 8,000	7	56,000
T	Balance = 24,000	(÷ 3) 8,000	6	48,000
	40,000			104,000

14: Limiting factor analysis

The profit-maximising product mix might not be possible because the mix is also restricted by a factor other than a scarce resource.

In such circumstances the organisation might have to produce more of a particular product or products than the level established by ranking according to contribution per unit of limiting factor.

Although 'single limiting factor analysis where a company has restricted freedom of action' is the specific syllabus content for Paper 8, the May 2001 question on limiting factor analysis did not involve this restriction.

Factors that restrict freedom of action

- A contract to supply a certain number of products

- Provision of a complete product range and/or maintenance of customer goodwill

- Maintenance of a certain market share

Basic approach

1. Rank the products in the normal way.

2. Take account of the minimum production requirements within the optimum production plan.

3. Allocate the remaining resources according to the ranking.

In the earlier example about L Ltd, suppose that the company has contracted to supply 9,000 units of T to an important customer. Here is the revised optimum sales/production plan.

Product	Hours	Production	Contribution per unit £	Total contribution £
T	(9,000 × 3) = 27,000	9,000	6	54,000
J	balance = 13,000	(13,000 ÷ 2) = 6,500	7	45,500
	40,000			99,500

An examination question is highly unlikely to tell you that an organisation has a 'restricted freedom of action'. Instead, look out for hints such as 'contracted to supply ...', 'minimum to be produced ...' and so on.

Suppose a company must subcontract work to make up a shortfall in its own production capacity.

Its total costs are minimised if those units bought have the lowest extra variable cost of buying per unit of scarce resource saved.

Example

A company, which makes three products, has limited labour time available.

	A	B	C
	£	£	£
Variable cost of making	10	16	14
Variable cost of buying	19	20	19
Extra variable cost of buying	9	4	5
Labour hours saved by buying (per unit)	3	2	2
Extra variable cost of buying per hour saved	£3	£2	£2.50
Priority for making in-house	1st	3rd	2nd

Opportunity cost

This represents the benefits foregone by using a limiting factor in one way instead of the next most profitable way.

Example

In the example on page 129, the opportunity cost of making J instead of more units of T is £2 per labour hour (T's contribution per labour hour).

If more labour hours were made available, more units of T (up to 10,000) would be made and an extra contribution of £2 per labour hour could be earned.

Similarly if fewer labour hours were available, fewer units of T would be made, production of J being kept at 8,000 units.

The loss of labour hours would cost the company £2 per labour hour in lost contribution.

Shadow price

A shadow price is the increase in contribution which would be created by having available one additional unit of a limiting resource at its normal variable cost.

This **lost contribution** (which is the marginal-earning potential of the limiting factor at the profit-maximising output level), is the **internal opportunity cost** or **shadow price** (or **dual price**) of the limiting factor.

Assumptions in limiting factor analysis

- Fixed costs will be the same whatever decision is taken.

- Unit variable costs are constant for all quantities of output.

- Sales demand is known with certainty.

- Resource requirements are known with certainty.

- Units of output are divisible.

Further considerations

- How much will sales demand be affected by changes in sales price, and how interdependent are sales of different products?

- Customer loyalty may be adversely affected by the business ceasing to produce a product.

- Competitors may take over vacated markets.

- It may not be possible to restart production of the product if labour skills have been lost.

- Further research may indicate the limiting factor is only limiting because of problems with the production process.

- Managers may want to achieve a satisfactory mix rather than a profit-maximising product mix in order to maintain employee goodwill.

Topic List

Linear programming

Formulating the problem

Shadow prices

Linear programming is a technique for allocating scarce resources so as to maximise profit or minimise costs. It can be applied to problems with the following features.

- *A **single objective** to maximise or minimise the value of a certain function*
- *Several **constraints**, typically scarce resources, that limit the value of the objective function*

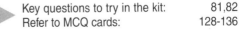

Key questions to try in the kit: 81,82
Refer to MCQ cards: 128-136

Linear programming

A technique for allocating scarce resources so as to maximise profit or minimise costs

Which technique to use

Number of products	Number of scarce resources	Technique
Any number	1	Limiting factor analysis
2	Any number	Graphical approach to linear programming
3 or more	Any number	Simplex approach to linear programming (covered in Paper 9)

This example will be used throughout the chapter.

Example

Suppose a company makes two products. Relevant data are as follows.

	Standard	Deluxe	Availability per month
Contribution per unit	£15	£20	
Labour hours per unit	5	10	4,000
Kgs of material per unit	10	5	4,250

Find the production plan which will maximise contribution.

1 Define variables

- Let x = number of standard produced each month
- Let y = number of deluxe produced each month

2 Establish objective function

Maximise contribution $(C) = 15x + 20y$ subject to the following constraints

3 Establish constraints

- Labour: $5x + 10y \leq 4,000$
- Material: $10x + 5y \leq 4,250$
- Non negativity: $x \geq 0, y \geq 0$

> Students often have problems with constraints of the style 'the quantity of one type must not exceed twice that of the other'. This can be interpreted as follows: the quantity of one type (say X) must not exceed (must be less than or equal to) twice that of the other (2Y) (ie $X \leq 2Y$).

4 **Graph the problem**

- Labour: $5x + 10y = 4,000$; if $x = 0$, $y = 400$, and if $y = 0$, $x = 800$

- Material: $10x + 5y = 4,250$; if $x = 0$, $y = 850$, and if $y = 0$, $x = 425$

5 **Define feasible area/region**

This is the area where *all* inequalities are satisfied (area above x axis and y axis ($x \geq 0$, $y \geq 0$), below material constraint ($\leq$) *and* below labour constraint ($\leq$)).

If you have to draw a graph make sure that it has a title, that the axes are labelled and that the constraint lines and feasible area are clearly identified.

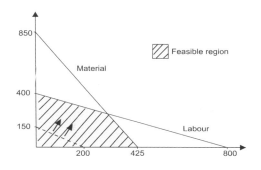

6 Determine optimal solution

Method 1

- Add an iso-contribution line (suppose C = £3,000 so that if C = 15x + 20y, then if x = 0, y = 150, and if y = 0, x = 200).

- (Sliding your ruler across the page if necessary) find the point furthest from the origin but still in the feasible area.

- Use simultaneous equations to find out the x and y coordinates at the optimal solution, the intersection of the material and labour constraints (x = 300, y = 250)(or find them directly from the graph).

Method 2

- Determine all possible intersection points of constraints and axes using simultaneous equations.

- Calculate contribution at each intersection point to determine which is the optimal solution.

Minimisation problems

- If the objective were to minimise costs the optimal solution would be at the point in the feasible area closest to the origin.

If the iso-contribution line is exactly parallel to one of the constraint lines there will not be a single optimum solution, but a range of solutions along the part of the line within the feasible area.

The extra contribution or profit that may be earned by relaxing by one unit a binding resource constraint

- Shadow prices are calculated on the basis that the extra available resource costs the normal variable amount.
- Shadow prices represent the maximum premium above the normal variable amount that an organisation should be willing to pay for one extra unit of a resource.
- Since shadow prices indicate the effect of a one unit change in a constraint, they provide a measure of the sensitivity of a result.
- The shadow price of a constraint that is not binding at the optimal solution is zero.
- Shadow prices are only valid for a small range before the constraint becomes non-binding or different resources become critical.
- Shadow prices enable management to make better informed decisions about payment of overtime premium, bonuses, premiums on small orders of raw materials etc.

You will not be required to calculate shadow prices in the exam.

15: Linear programming (graphical)

Notes

16: Multiple product CVP analysis

Topic List

Breakeven point

C/S ratio

Sales/product mix decisions

Target profits and margin of safety

Multi-product CVP charts

*It is vital to remember that for multiple product CVP analysis, a **constant product sales mix** (whenever x units of product A are sold, y units of product B and z units of product C are also sold) must be **assumed**.*

Key question to try in the kit: 80,89-93
Refer to MCQ cards: 137-150

Example (J Ltd) used throughout this chapter (where appropriate)

J Ltd produces and sells two products

- The M sells for £7 per unit and has a total variable cost of £3 per unit.
- The N sells for £15 per unit an.d has a total variable cost of £5 per unit.

For every five units of M sold, one unit of N will be sold.

Fixed costs total £30,000.

You need to be completely confident of the aspects of CVP (breakeven) analysis covered in your foundation level studies.

CVP analysis has been examined in the MCQ section of every exam to date.

How to calculate a multi-product breakeven point

1. Calculate the contribution per unit.
2. Calculate the contribution per mix.
3. Calculate the breakeven point in number of mixes.
4. Calculate the breakeven point in units and revenue.

Example (J Ltd)

1. M = £4   N = £10

2. (£4 × 5) + (£10 × 1) = £30

3. Fixed costs ÷ contribution per mix
   = £30,000 ÷ £30 = 1,000 mixes

4. M 1,000 × 5 = 5,000 units
       5,000 × £7 = £35,000 revenue

   N 1,000 × 1 = 1,000 units
       1,000 × £15 = £15,000 revenue

   Total breakeven revenue = £50,000

16: Multiple product CVP analysis

How to calculate a multi-product C/S (or profit volume or P/V) ratio

Calculation of breakeven sales: approach 1

1 Calculate the revenue per mix.

2 Calculate the contribution per mix.

3 Calculate the average C/S ratio.

4 Calculate the total breakeven point.

5 Calculate the revenue ratio per mix.

6 Calculate the breakeven sales.

Example

1 $(£7 \times 5) + (£15 \times 1) = £50$

2 $(£4 \times 5) + (£10 \times 1) = £30$

3 $(£30 \div £50) \times 100\% = 60\%$

4 Fixed costs $\div$ C/S ratio $= £30,000 \div 0.6$ $= £50,000$

5 $(£7 \times 5) : (£15 \times 1) = 35 : 15$ or $7 : 3$

6 M $= £50,000 \times 7/10 = £35,000$
   N $= £50,000 \times 3/10 = \underline{£15,000}$
   $\underline{\underline{£50,000}}$

Calculation of breakeven sales: approach 2

You may just be provided with individual C/S ratios.

Example

C/S ratio of X = 45%

C/S ratio of Y = 35%

Ratio of sales = 3:4

$$\text{Average C/S ratio} = \frac{(45\% \times 3) + (35\% \times 4)}{7}$$

$$= 39.3\%$$

You can then carry on from step **4** above.

Target contributions

Example (J Ltd)

J Ltd wishes to earn contribution of £500,000.

Sales revenue = (£1 ÷ C/S ratio) × £500,000
= (£1 ÷ 0.6*) × £500,000 = £833,333

* from example on page 146

Any change in the proportions of products in the mix will change the contribution per mix and the average C/S ratio and hence the breakeven point.

16: Multiple product CVP analysis

Most profitable mix option

Suppose J Ltd (from our example) has the option of changing the sales ratio to 2M to 4N. Which is the optimal mix?

1. Calculate breakeven point in number of mixes.   2. Calculate breakeven point in units and revenue.

Example (J Ltd)

1. Mix 1: 1,000 mixes (calculated on page 145)
   Mix 2: Contribution per mix = (£4 × 2) + (£10 × 4)
   = £48
   Breakeven point = £30,000 ÷ £48
   = 625 mixes

2. Mix 1: £50,000 (calculated on page 145)
   Mix 2: M   625 × 2 = 1,250 units
         1,250 × £7 = £8,750 units
       N   625 × 4 = 2,500 units
         2,500 × £15 = £37,500 revenue
   Total breakeven revenue = £46,250

Mix 2 is preferable because it requires a lower level of sales to break even (because it has a higher average contribution per unit sold of £48/6 = £8 (compared with £30/6 = £5 for mix 1).

Changing the product mix

ABC Ltd sells products Alpha and Beta in the ratio 5:1 at the same selling price per unit. Beta has a C/S ratio of 66.67% and the overall C/S ratio is 58.72%. How do we calculate the overall C/S ratio if the mix is changed to 2:5?

1 Calculate the missing C/S ratio

- Calculate original market share (Alpha 5/6, Beta 1/6).
- Calculate weighted C/S ratios.
  - Beta: $0.6667 \times 0.1667 = 0.1111$
  - Alpha: $0.5872 - 0.1111 = 0.4761$
- Calculate the missing C/S ratio.

	Alpha	Beta	Total
C/S ratio	0.5713 *	0.6667	
Market share	× 0.8333	× 0.1667	
	0.4761	0.1111	0.5872

* 0.4761/0.8333

2 Calculate the revised overall C/S ratio

	Alpha	Beta	Total
C/S ratio (as in 1)	0.5713	0.6667	
Market share (2/7:5/7)	× 0.2857	× 0.7143	
	0.1632	0.4762	0.6394

> The overall C/S ratio has increased because of the increase in the proportion of the mix of the Beta, which has the higher C/S ratio.

Target profits: approach 1

1 Calculate the contribution per mix.

2 Calculate the required number of mixes.

3 Calculate the required number of units and sales revenue of each product.

> You should remember from your foundation level studies that the contribution required to earn a target profit (P) = fixed costs + P.

Example (J Ltd)

Suppose J Ltd wishes to earn profit of £24,900.

1 £30 (as on page 145)

2 (Fixed costs + required profit)/contribution per mix = £(30,000 + 24,900)/£30 = 1,830 mixes

3
	£
M: (1,830 × 5) units for (× £7)	64,050
N: (1,830 × 1) units for (× £15)	27,450
Total revenue	91,500
Variable costs (9,150 × £3) + (1,830 × £5)	36,600
Fixed costs	30,000
Profit	24,900

Target profits: approach 2

1. Calculate the average C/S ratio.
2. Calculate the required total revenue.

Example (J Ltd)

1. 60% (from page 146)
2. Required contribution ÷ C/S ratio
   = (fixed costs + profit) ÷ C/S ratio
   = £54,900 ÷ 0.6 = £91,500

Margin of safety

1. Calculate the breakeven point in revenue.
2. Calculate the margin of safety.

Example (J Ltd)

Suppose J Ltd has budgeted sales of £62,000.

1. £50,000 (from page 145)
2. Budgeted sales – breakeven sales
   = £(62,000 – 50,000) = £12,000
   = 19.4% of budgeted sales

16: Multiple product CVP analysis

Breakeven chart

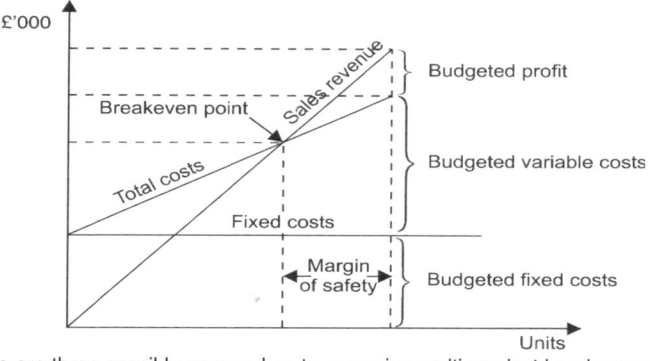

A multi-product breakeven chart can only be drawn on the assumption that the sales proportions are fixed.

There are three possible approaches to preparing multi-product breakeven charts.

- Output in £ sales and a constant product mix
- Products in sequence
- Output in tems of % of forecast sales and a constant product mix

P/V chart

Suppose J Ltd's sales budget is 6,000 units of M and 1,200 units of N.

Revenue (6,000 × £7 + 1,200 × £15) = £60,000

Variable costs (6,000 × £3 + 1,200 × £5) = £24,000

On the chart, products are shown individually, from left to right, in order of size of decreasing C/S ratio.

	C/S ratio	Cum sales £'000	Cum profit £'000
N	66.67%	18	*(18)
M	57.14%	60	6

* (1,200 × £15) – (12,000 × £5) – £30,000

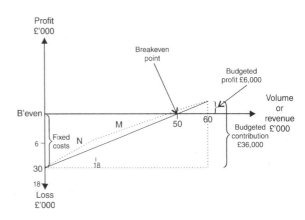

What the multi-product P/V chart highlights

- The overall company breakeven point

- Which products should be expanded in output (the most profitable in terms of C/S ratio) and which, if any, should be discontinued

- What effect changes in selling price and sales revenue would have on breakeven point and profit

- The average profit (the solid line which joins the two ends of the dotted line) earned from the sales of the products in the mix